FIRE UPON
THE EARTH

FIRE UPON THE EARTH

Interior Castle Explored

St. Teresa's Teaching on the Life
of Deep Union with God

Ruth Burrows

Dimension Books · Denville, New Jersey

Published by Dimension Books, Inc.
Denville, New Jersey 07834

Contents

Acknowledgements

The author and publishers are grateful to the following for permission to use extracts from works published by them:

Burns & Oates Ltd, for *Complete Works of St John of the Cross* edited by E. Allison Peers.

Cambridge University Press, for *The Interpretation of the Fourth Gospel* by C.H. Dodd.

Darton Longman & Todd Ltd, for *Love's Endeavour, Love's Expense* by William Vanstone.

Faber & Faber Ltd, for *Report to Greco* by Nikos Kazantzakis.

Introduction

If I succeed in my aim, this book will have a twofold character; it will indeed be a commentary on St Teresa's *Interior Castle*, and someone should be able to read that work slowly, turn to this one and find every important point elucidated; at the same time, if it is a true re-presentation of that classic, then it should stand in its own right as a useful guide to a life of union with God.

I cannot imagine how any thoughtful reader could fail to be impressed by St Teresa's writings even though he does not find them attractive, even though he finds himself bewildered, perhaps 'put off'. They ring with authenticity. Here is a woman who surely *knows*. She isn't merely speculating, deducing; she isn't relying on what others have said. Here is one with a well of living knowledge within her and it is from this she is drawing all the time. Her complete certainty is overwhelming, (and that in spite of the inevitable emotional insecurity that must attend our mortal state), she knows, she is certain, that what Jesus was proclaiming, what Paul, John and others have tried to express of man's ultimate destiny of being with Christ in God, one spirit with him who is Spirit, has become, even in this life, a living reality in her. For her, it is no longer a matter of being called to it, being on the way to it. For her it has happened; the kingdom of God has come in her in its overpowering, transforming truth, and she tells us, as John of the Cross will likewise tell us, that this is true of few in their earthly sojourn. Teresa is aware that she has a living knowledge known to few and that she is called to communicate this knowledge to others: a wholly new dimension of human existence which can never be known theoretically but only by moving into it and living there. It is that which eye has not seen, nor ear heard and what the heart of man

1

cannot conceive. Nevertheless, we can set our feet firmly on the path that leads to this wisdom – and what else is life for? – a path that, because of our human pride which blinds us, is not an obvious one.

We cannot afford to dismiss witnesses to the truth of our human existence, truth which is literally a matter of life and death, simply because they don't happen to suit our taste, don't click with us, and allow us to feel perfectly justified in turning to those more congenial to us and, most probably, less challenging. There are not many such witnesses to the sheer meaning of life; at least there are not many who have been endowed, as Teresa was, with the ability to look at, analyse and describe, the growing process of their life in Christ. Surely it is our duty to wrestle with their modes of expression, struggling to extract the shining, basic truth from what, because it has all the reality of a particular human experience, written in a particular climate of ideas and literary forms, is inevitably obscure at times and even misleading.

Because I am deeply convinced of the enormous importance of Teresa's teaching, and that few, if any, have spoken with greater knowledge (let alone the fact that, as a Carmelite, I am bound to a close study of her who embodies the charism of our order) that I have, over long years, tried to understand and learn from her. Initially I had difficulties to overcome. For one thing, she wasn't 'my cup of tea', as we say, though now I find her more to my taste simply because I understand her better. But then I was up against a bigger problem. In common with all my brothers and sisters in the order, I was conditioned to regard her with awe, as our 'seraphic Mother' whose every word almost, was inspired. Anecdote on anecdote led one to think that her teaching came direct from God, particularly that of the *Interior Castle*. Why, she was seen in ecstasy as she wrote it and she herself suggests that what she wrote seems to have been 'given' rather than come from herself! What temerity then to suggest that perhaps now and then she was mistaken; or even that she did not express herself clearly and was not always consistent! Dare one question that perhaps the intellectual, theological, literary tools available were often inadequate and clumsy for what she was trying to communicate. Such thinking could bring seraphic Teresa down into the same inadequate, unsatisfactory, humdrum world as ourselves. I speak of many years ago and what I say may well cause my modern reader to smile. But the difficulty was real enough to me and had to be mastered. Jesus was my answer as he is the answer to everything. 'The servant is not greater than the Master'. To accept Jesus is to accept the human situation fully; it is to accept history, that each of us is in history and therefore conditioned, as he was, by our times, the climate of ideas, the prejudices and so forth. Why should Tersa be a seraph when Jesus was not? 'We are not angels', she herself roundly proclaims, 'but men'.

Jesus' inner knowledge transcended every possible expression even to himself. Is this too hard for us to grasp? It seems beyond doubt that he expected the end of the world very soon, possibly with his own death and this because of his vivid awareness that God was acting in him, working a tremendous work through him. The end of the world has not yet come. Was Jesus mistaken? In a superficial sense, yes; in the deepest sense, absolutely no. His insight was of the depth of God, of the depth of God's dealing with and purpose for man. Jesus spoke from a depth he himself could not be fully aware of, could not fully translate into human concepts, and when he tried to, of necessity it was within the totally inadequate images, thought patterns and expectancies of his time. This was part of the reality of his humanness. To deny this to him is to deny his humanity. What he *knew* was utter truth, and what he uttered was utter truth in its deepest meaning. What more true than in his death and resurrection the world came to an end? This world order crumbles and falls apart and a new one comes into existence. The kingdom of God comes in power as the kingdom of this world is overthrown. We can't think in terms of the collective when we are dealing with such profound realities. The kingdom of God comes only insofar as it comes into individuals. The human heart must receive it otherwise it does not come. To receive this kingdom the old world in us must have been overthrown. To receive the kingdom we must be born again in the travails of birth. To live the new life we must die to the old. Truly the end of the world has come.

The coming of the kingdom into the individual heart, the great earthquake, the overturning of this world order in the Easter event, is what Teresa's teaching is all about. It may seem banal to say it is what she, and John of the Cross mean by supernatural or mystical prayer. Hackneyed, technical, ugly words for the most profound thing that can happen to a creature.

It is a passage from this world 'to the Father', a moving into a wholly new world. When this happens, then our world has come to an end, the world of 'flesh' bounded by our material being and its inability to enter the kingdom of the Father.

Here I seem to be killing two birds with one stone: on the one hand preparing my readers for an unabashed, critical but intensely admiring search into Teresa's writings, and an interpretation in modern terms; and, on the other, at the very outset, heralding the theme of this book that what Teresa is talking about is the very heart of Jesus' own revelation. It is the profoundest reality of our existence as human beings.

The substance of this commentary came into being as, on Sunday evenings in winter, my sisters in Carmel, would in their humility, come to listen to my attempts to explore the mansions. Their response encouraged me. The ideas have been worked over constantly, some of them expressed anew to a younger audience for whom the subject matter was entirely novel. It is to my community, both those who are my companions and friends of long years and the newcomers equally dear, that this book is offered with love and gratitude. It is offered too, to all my brothers and sisters in Carmel as we prepare to celebrate the fourth centenary of Teresa's death. There are many others also to whom I owe gratitude for what they have shared with me and who have helped me to clarify and deepen my insights. To them also I offer this book with affection.

What is Teresa herself thinking of this attempt of mine? I feel confident on one score and that is that she enjoys my constant curiosity with her castle and my explorations. 'Considering how strictly cloistered you are, my sisters how few opportunities you have for recreation . . . I think it will be a great consolation for you . . . to take your delight in this interior castle, for you can walk about in it at any time without asking leave from your superiors.' What is more, she liked her daughters to be daring in love, willingly to take risks and not be afraid of looking foolish. This book, whatever its merits or demerits, springs from love. I think I hear her saying, ''Pon my soul, daughter', (or the Spanish equivalent), 'you certainly have had a good try!'

First Mansion

Every time I read the first few paragraphs of the *Interior Castle* I am struck anew by the beauty of them. Behind these glowing words is an impassioned heart pouring out its praise, love and gratitude, trying to awaken others to the blazing reality in which she already lives and in which we too can live, for it is our destiny. Teresa herself seems to have been enchanted with the image of the crystal castle, this 'orient pearl', so 'beautiful and resplendent'. She declared to a friend that it was not of her devising but was given to her in a vision. This 'celestial building which is within us' is our soul, alas, 'so little understood by mortals!' It is composed of a vast number of rooms, above, below, around, and in the innermost chamber dwells the king. Is it any wonder that the 'dwelling of such a King, so mighty, so pure and so full of all that is good' be lovely beyond compare? After all, is not our soul made in the very image of God?

We find ourselves somewhat embarrassed by Teresa's dualistic notion of soul and body – '. . . we are living in these bodies . . . we possess souls'; the body is only the 'rough setting of the diamond' or the 'outer wall of the castle'. But it need not worry us. Conditioned as she was by the thinking of her times, as we are by ours, she could not have expressed herself otherwise.

What we have to do is see what Teresa is really saying about the soul. She is saying that it is *for God*; it is a capacity for God; he is its centre and all its beauty is because of him. This soul, this castle of immeasurable beauty and capacity is ourselves. It is there, this wonder, inviting exploration and possession even to the innermost room 'where the most secret things pass between God and the soul' and we are content to stay in the outer courts, if we choose to enter at all! For her, spiritual growth is seen as a journey inwards, a penetration of this interior castle. In her understanding, the castle is *already there*, our souls are, so to speak, *ready made*, we have only to get to know them by entering in. There is a problem but she avoids it by not seeing it! But to say that we are not yet in our castle, at least not in any but the outer-most court, is really saying the mansions are *not there yet*, they come into existence. So important is this insight, which Teresa grasped *practically* but did not express clearly in her use of a static image, for understanding what she calls the 'supernatural work' of God and later calls infused or mystical contemplation, to expound which, is her reason for writing the book, that we must enlarge upon it.

Man, to use the classical expression, is a capacity for God. Unlike every other form of life that we know of, he does not come into the world ready made. The baby animal is animal, whole and entire. It grows, reaches maturity and fulfilment within the bounds of its own being and the world around it. The human creature, this being made up of the same stuff as the world and thrown up by its evolution, is not ready made. It comes into the world incomplete, with no possibility of completion within itself or within the bounds of the material world. It is a capacity, a possibility; a capacity that may never be filled, a possibility that may never be realised, for, in this instance, the creature has a choice. Man is a capacity for God, he comes into existence insofar as he consents to be what he is, a 'for-Godness'. The human being is not a man until the possibility which he is, is totally realized, the capacity which he is, expanded to its limits, 'filled with all the fulness of God'. Man, we maintain, *is not there yet*. In Teresa's imagery, the mansions aren't there yet, just the foundation stones. They are to be built by the Master builder insofar as we consent to work with him.

Had Teresa any idea when she thought of her *moradas*, consciously quoting the text of John 14:2, of an old interpretation of this scripture text? *Mŏnē*, usually translated as mansion or dwelling place, can equally mean a staging-inn, a place where travellers may stop for a while as they journey. Such stopping places would be along frequented routes. Jesus could well be saying that, 'with my Father, there are many such staging-inns. I am going away to make it possible for you to use them all, to pass from one to another until you reach the "dwelling place" where I am, the Father's heart.'

The idea that we are not there yet, that we have to become – shall we say, I have to become *me* and my *me* has to become God – finds firm basis in scripture in its talk of being born anew, a new creation, something wholly new and other coming into existence. The concept of the distinction between spirit and flesh is particularly important for our theme. For both Paul and John, 'flesh' seems to indicate simply 'what is not God'. Thus the human being in itself is 'flesh'. 'Spirit' stands for the God-realm. God is spirit, he alone can communicate spirit and what he touches becomes spirit. Never can 'flesh' mount up to reach 'spirit', 'spirit' stoops down to touch 'flesh', quickening it with new, 'spiritual' life, which is the life of God himself. 'What is born of the flesh is flesh' – flesh can never generate spirit – 'what is born of spirit is spirit'. 'It is spirit that gives life, flesh is good for nothing'. Flesh and blood cannot penetrate the mysteries of God. All that can be said of man who is 'flesh' is that he is open to spirit, he has the capacity to be touched by and transformed into spirit, becoming one spirit with the Lord who is Spirit. His whole destiny lies in being born again into spirit. When, in this book, we speak of 'spirit' and 'spiritual', it is always with the meaning given here unless indicated. We are never allowing an opposition between soul and body. When we use spirit, or soul, (we choose to use them synonymously though Teresa makes a distinction between the two words) we mean the whole person insofar as they have been touched by God and are being transformed into spirit. It is only when flesh has become spirit totally that we have man. If man chooses to remain flesh, as can easily happen, he remains a shrivelled parody of humanness, like an aborted embryo. When Jesus tells us that we must become as children, is this what he is meaning? John in his story of Jesus and Nicodemus seems to say that Jesus wants us to grasp that, though we think of ourselves as grownup men and women, knowledgeable, versed even in religious matters, we are not yet there, we are incomplete, undeveloped, like infants. Even less than that, says Jesus to Nicodemus. You have yet to be born!

8

It should readily be understood that God's communication of himself is according to the capacity that is there to receive him. His love still embraces the aborted embryo, humbly offering itself, but the poor thing simply hasn't the capacity to realize it, let alone respond. Surely it is impossible that anyone, ever, has remained so totally closed, that not in one single instance, has it responded. And every response, no matter how feeble, means a becoming.

In the very first verses of the bible we read of the Spirit of God brooding over the dark waters of chaos and calling things into being. This primal theme runs through the bible: our God is a giving, communicating God. He calls into existence what is not and calls into fuller existence what is. He calls the winds, the waves, the stars. He gives himself to everything that is according to its capacity to receive him, be it the grass and flowers of the field, the poor worm, the kingly beast or man. Only man has the power to respond to God, consciously to answer the call. This ability to hear the call and to answer it, is what makes man man. I found keen delight in a poem by Nikos Kazantzakis, a Cretan poet. I do not know his beliefs but, as it stands, the poem wonderfully expresses what I believe.

Blowing through the heaven and earth, and in our hearts and in the heart of every living thing, is a gigantic breath – a great Cry – which we call God. Plant life wished to continue its motionless sleep next to stagnant waters, but the Cry leaped up within it and violently shook its roots: 'Away, let go of the earth, walk!' Had the tree been able to think and judge, it would have cried, 'I don't want to. What are you urging me to do? You are demanding the impossible!'

But the Cry, without pity, kept shaking its roots and shouting, 'Away! Let go of the earth, walk!'

It shouted in this way for thousands of eons; and lo, as a result of desire and struggle, life escaped the motionless tree and was liberated.

Animals appeared – worms – making themselves at home in water and mud. 'We're just fine', they said, 'We have peace and security; we're not budging'.

But the terrible cry hammered itself pitilessly into their loins.

'Leave the mud, stand up, give birth to your betters!'

9

'We don't want to! We can't!'

'You can't, but I can! Stand up!'

And lo! after thousands of eons, man emerged trembling on his still unsolid legs.

The human being is a centaur; his equine hoofs are planted in the ground, but the body from breast to head is worked on and tormented by the merciless Cry. He has been fighting, again for thousands of eons, to draw himself out of this animalistic scabbard. He is also fighting – and this is his new struggle – to draw himself out of his human scabbard. Man calls in despair 'Where can I go? I have reached the pinnacle, beyond is the abyss'. And the Cry answers, 'I am beyond. Stand up!'

Man is the being to whom God cries, 'Come to me'. 'Come, take possession of the kingdom prepared for you before the foundation of the world.' It was for this the world was made, that there should be beings capable of receiving God, entering into closest fellowship with him, sharing all God is and has.

'Blessed be the God and Father of our Lord Jesus Christ . . . who has blessed us in Christ with every spiritual blessing in the heavenly places. He chose us in him before the foundation of the world that we should be holy . . . He destined us in love to be his sons through Jesus Christ . . . Those whom he foreknew he also predestined to be conformed to the image of his Son in order that he might be the firstborn of many brethren. And those whom he predestined, he also called, and those whom he called, he also justified; and those whom he justified, he also glorified.'

The call 'Come to me' is not an afterthought as though God first made man and then decided to call him to intimacy with himself. This divine call is what constitutes man.

In our image of organic growth, as, say, the seed evolves into the tree, the crysalis into the butterfly, how do we explain Teresa's certitude that God dwells in the centre of the soul? There is an anecdote of how Teresa came by her image of the castle. She confided to a friend in an unguarded hour, that it been given to her through a vision when she was longing for some insight 'into the beauty of a soul in grace'. Now, by her own testimony she was already dwelling in the seventh

10

mansion when she wrote her book, *The Interior Castle*. We will have occasion later to point out that Teresa's insight into the workings of God in the soul were always personal. May we not conclude that her vision was not of soul in general but of her own soul, her own transformed being? By this time she had reached full spiritual growth. What, in her as in us all, has at the outset been mere potentiality, has now become reality under the constant action of God and her own surrender to this action. Truly the 'King of Glory' dwelt in her, in the greatest splendour' 'illumining and beautifying' her whole being. She gives us an idea of what God will do in a surrendered heart. This is the state of grace properly so called, and only at this stage of full growth can the term 'indwelling' be used in full truth.

We would be totally mistaken, however, were we to conclude from this that until we reach the seventh mansion we cannot think of God and pray to him as within us or close to us. It can never be said too often that God is always present, always bestowing himself in the measure that he can be received. On his side it is total gift, it is on our side that the check lies. Teresa is aware of this. She expresses the initial lack of intimacy between ourselves and God as due to the noise, the junk and the pernicious reptiles invading the outer courts of the castle where we are. Thus it is that we can't hear the voice of the king within nor can we catch his radiant light which is ever streaming. We would express it by saying we are too small to receive much of God, too undeveloped to be intimate with him. God continually offers intimacy, permeating our being as he permeates all that is. It is his most passionate desire that this constant, caring, nurturing become an indwelling of intimacy. At any moment, therefore, we can turn to our loving God who is closer to us than we are to ourselves. From the very outset, in our embryonic state, we are 'so richly endowed as to have the power to hold converse with none other than God himself'. This is what makes us human beings.

There are two points to touch on before we pass on. One is Teresa's use of the term 'mansions'. She is not wholly consistent here. Undoubtedly her fundamental meaning and the one she maintains throughout, is that there are stages of growth; we pass from one mansion to another, always inward, until we reach the last, central chamber. It is well to note, however, that occasionally it has a different meaning. She sometimes uses it to describe the different kinds of 'favours' the Lord bestows; again, to refer to the different topics of meditations we may employ, as in these early chapters '. . . it (the soul) must be allowed to roam through these mansions . . . it must not be compelled to remain for long in one single room . . .' Clearly we cannot move from stage to stage at will!

The second is the question of 'favours'. We cannot escape this problem for long. From the start we are faced with it. Teresa seems to be offering us plums! It would not be honest or helpful to insist that she has in mind the great, essential favour of growing union with God. For her, this seems inextricably bound up with 'favours', 'consolations'. This is not the place to discuss them but we shall do so later on. I don't want to jeopardize the confidence of my readers by a preliminary, airy dismissal. Nevertheless, that being said, we are absolutely justified in interpreting her fulsome promises as that of growing union with God which is the supreme blessedness. Teresa would be the first to affirm this interpretation. In spite of her enthusiasm for 'favours', Teresa could yet declare them relatively unimportant. They come and go, we cannot be absolutely certain of their origin. They are of value only insofar as they foster the supreme favour and consolation – union with God. The antithesis of the 'state of grace' is the state of sin. Teresa recounted to her friend that, following the radiant vision of the soul 'in a state of grace', she was shown what its condition would be were it to 'fall into mortal sin'. 'No thicker darkness exists, and there is nothing dark or black that is not much less so than this'; but the overwhelmingly important truth for her is that God has not withdrawn from the soul. Whatever she learned from doctrinal instructions, her heart was certain that God never withdraws in anger, never forsakes. It is we who turn our backs on him, we who shut ourselves off from his light. So vivid is her awareness of the for-Godness of man, that sin is a distortion of being by which he becomes unnatural, like a tree, uprooted by its own will from the life-giving springs, and

12

choosing to plant itself in 'a pool of pitch-black, evil-smelling water', bearing not leaves and fruit but only 'misery and filth'.

The essence of sin is the refusal to respond to God's summons to become, to receive the only real life which he wishes to give. It is choosing to stay 'flesh'. When we think of the response to God's call, we must not imagine an important, solid reality, walking on firm legs towards him. The image is rather that of a seed responding to the call of spring. 'Come up, little Pip, come up, little Pip!' as once I heard a teacher sing to her class of children during a nature lesson. The seed 'comes' insofar as it 'becomes', sending down its tap root, thrusting its growing point above the soil, unfolding its sepals, petals and leaves. It is our terrible ability to refuse to become. Unlike the worms in water and mud, we can truly refuse, 'I'm not budging, I have peace and security where I am, in my mud'. Yet here we are, talking as if there were an 'I' to make this refusal. The 'I' only comes into being in answer to the call. When we grasp that self is *mere potentiality*, something of our total dependency on God is forced upon us. It is a revelation most painful to human pride and yet the acceptance of this lies at the heart of all true growth. It is in the light of this imperative for man to recognize his true condition, that one can see blessed meaning in the afflictions, frustrations and ever-present curtailments and disappointments which are his lot. Without these, would we ever come anywhere near to a sense of truth?

If we know Teresa's writings well we shall often have been puzzled by her strange notions of sin. It seems, for one thing, that she thought it quite an easy matter to commit a mortal sin and this in spite of the fact that the effect of mortal sin was catastrophic. To die in mortal sin was to be damned for ever. Here we see Teresa intellectually dependent on the doctrinal teaching current in her day. Doubtless she had been instructed in the neat distinctions between mortal and venial sins: the former severed all friendship with God, 'killing' the soul; the latter weakened the friendship but did not destroy it. Again, she would have been taught the conditions necessary for a sin to be mortal: grave matter, full consent, full knowledge. The odd thing is, to our way of thinking, that Teresa, in her estimation of

13

mortal sin, overlooked the first condition, grave matter. This is another instance of where her heart, closely united with our Lord's, broke out of the intellectual system. Teresa, an original thinker, has to rely on the intellectual tools at hand to express herself, and these tools are often inadequate. Her insights force her beyond them – just a slight adaptation and the whole nuance is different. Thus she is easily misread; we do not realize that she is saying something new. Surely it is because of her union with God that Teresa's view of sin does not fit into legalistic categories. These latter are theories and may have no relation to reality for they do not belong to the area of personal relationship. We are wise to bypass them and think of sin in terms of love. Then it becomes clear that it is not wrong acts that matter so much as wrong attitudes. A man may, technically, be faithful to his wife, but he neglects her, she might just as well not be there; love is dead. Another commits an infidelity and is deeply sorry. Love is not dead and the relationship need hardly be damaged, it can be strengthened by the lapse deeply repented of. We recall Peter's denial of Jesus, shameful and serious enough objectively speaking, but ultimately it didn't matter, it led to a deeper love.

Sin is 'the *mystery* of iniquity', as scripture says, precisely because it has everything to do with the mystery of a man's relationship to God. In this mystery of sin we find ourselves with no footholds, we have no certainties, no neat categories. No one can glibly think 'I have never committed a mortal sin', or, 'I have done so-and-so, but it is only a venial sin'. We may be right in the legalistic sense but that means nothing to God. Perhaps we have hardly noticed – because, of course, we did not want to notice – a profoundly selfish choice. It may have been in quite a small matter but it was the beginning of blindness. It may have been that, before this choice, there was a straight path to God before us, but at a certain point, with hardly a thought, we turned aside and henceforth settled for mediocrity. For any person who really prays, this could not be. The opposite can happen. We may recall with constant and bitter sorrow the commission of a grave sin, when knowingly, deliberately, we said 'no' to God. Yet, in reality, it may have

14

had no detrimental effect. The sorrow, humiliation and the resolution never to say 'no' again, have brought us very close to God.

The mystery of sin. Scripture gives us bewildering instances of it. Had Ananias and Sapphira a clear idea of the gravity of what they were doing? It seems not. How terrible the consequences! What does the legalist make of it? Look at Saul and David. I expect most of us have felt sympathy for Saul in his beginnings – his disobedience under stress seems understandable enough, and, after all, it was only once. Whereas David – adultery, murder, treachery ... God's judgments are not ours. He saw that Saul's apparently excusable act of disobedience revealed a total disregard of him, while David, in spite of his many grievous sins, remained a man of God, one for whom God always mattered.

The sheer mystery of sin, our sense of helplessness when we face its mysteriousness, can be a most powerful incentive for humility and trust in God, two things which, as we shall see, must constantly grow if we are to reach our end. Their importance cannot be stressed enough. We are all the time wanting to find ways of making ourselves safe, devising categories and measurements well within our compass which can give us an illusory sense of 'being alright', we know where we are. Whereas God has never given us such safeguards and securities. He calls always and always for our total trust in him alone. We are always wanting to protect ourselves from him by these and other means; he gives us no *thing* whatever in which to trust – only himself. We are blessed if we really accept that we do not know whether we are worthy of ourselves of praise or blame, when we refuse to summon any legalism to our defense but stand humbly and trustfully as sinners before the Lord. We must bear the weight of our sinfulness and look for no relief save in the free, loving forgiveness of God. We have nothing good as of ourselves, Teresa declares from sheer experience. 'Without me you can do nothing', affirms our loving Lord. Over and over again Teresa will insist on our need for self-knowledge until the end of our life. The nearer we draw to God the more it will be ours without any labour. But in our beginnings, when his light cannot illumine us so strongly, we have to work to acquire it and what surer grounds for fostering true humble self-knowledge than consideration of the mystery of sin.

Is it really true that we 'offend' or 'displease' God? What do we mean by such expressions? Surely what we mean is that when we sin, that is, when we disobey his loving summons to fuller life, we tie God's hands. He cannot give us all he wants to give us; cannot make us happy as he wills. This is God's grief, this is how we 'offend' him. We can recall here Jesus' frustration and grief at the folly and obduracy of men refusing the blessedness God was offering through himself. 'How I forgot myself last night! I cannot think how it happened. These desires and this love of mine made me lose all sense of proportion . . .' Teresa exclaims the morning after her long, expansive chat with her friend when she told him of her vision of the soul. Undoubtedly she was more restrained when she had actually sat down to write her treatise on the Castle, nevertheless her passion blazes through. Here she is, all eagerness to communicate the sense of urgency that grips her, frustrated at our lethargy, our reluctance even to look at our castle; we won't take the trouble because we aren't interested. 'Souls without prayer are like people whose bodies or limbs are paralyzed: they possess feet and hands but they cannot control them'.

For one who has arrived even at the outer courts of the castle, prayer is taken for granted, for 'the door of entry into this castle is prayer and meditation'. Many of us in childhood would have learned by rote, 'prayer is the raising of the mind and heart to God', and this simple formula, though far from adequate, fits happily into our context. How can we know our destiny, how can we know what God would do for us, how can we desire it, unless we reflect? This is what Teresa begs us all to do or to make a start of doing if we have not already made one. Unless we are prepared to take this first step there is nothing she can do to help us. If only we can get inside, just inside the door even, and have a minimum of desire to go further, there is hope. For to know even a little of the love of God and his promises to us,

16

must enkindle some desire however feeble, and what is more, every step inwards brings us a little closer to the king whose closeness draws us further. As we would say, every little growth means there is more capacity to receive him. There is no other way of entering the castle, no other means of growth, save by prayer and meditation.

In these courts we are far too near the moat for comfort. Reptiles swarm in from the moat and sorely harass us if they do not harm us. Let us try to understand what Teresa means by these reptiles to which she often refers. 'Flesh' is not innocent, it is sinful; the desires of the flesh are clean contrary to spirit, they make war on it; flesh is coiled up on itself, warped with selfishness. What we pursue is our immediate, comprehensible gratification whether on the level of bodily need or those we like to deem more spiritual though in actual fact they are every bit as much sinful 'flesh': nothing more nor less than what scripture calls 'the lust of the flesh, the lust of the eyes, and the pride of life'. We feel we are serving our interests but we are not, we are working for our destruction. To choose to remain trapped 'flesh' is damnation. We have no meaning, no fulfilment save in opening ourselves to God, going out beyond ourselves to obey and love him. Only in responding to love do we become ourselves. If man would go out of himself in love, he must draw himself painfully out of 'his animalistic scabbard' as our poet has said. This means he has to struggle to ensure that his instincts, all that he has in common with the animals, are governed by his reason. Unchecked they run away with us and we are cruel, jealous, greedy, violent and so forth. We can never love until we control our passions. Great and constant effort is needed before we are free enough to give ourselves in dedicated service to others. Man, to be man, must be a servant; it is of his essence and this because it is of the essence of God to be servant, and we are to be like him. When God showed us his inmost nature, the way he is as God, he came to us in the form of a servant, and, 'as I have done, so you must do also'. Indulge our three lusts and we are left crawling on the earth, misshapen, shrivelled being akin to the reptiles, as Teresa would say. We can choose to be just like that or we can choose to become sons of God, transformed into Jesus.

Teresa spells out for us more than once the form these reptiles take – worldliness: absorption in worldly affairs, in its honours, ambitions and false values. She begs us to withdraw from such vanities and give time and trouble to what is for our everlasting blessedness: think of who we are, what we are for; think of the goodness of God, the promises to which he is pledged. We have to distinguish carefully, in a way Teresa never felt obliged to do in theory, between a true appreciation of the created world and human values which is essential if we would love God, for he is their author and loves all he has made, and a worldliness, the heart of which is selfishness. It is not the world that is harmful – quite the contrary – but our hearts, we poison what we touch. We 'lust', we want to possess, dominate, devour, destroy. Love serves.

There is always a danger for those of us already devoted to a spiritual life, of passing over what seems addressed to 'people in the world', that is, those still entangled with worldly things. Take religious, for instance. Have they not deliberately renounced the pursuit of worldly pleasures and ambitions? Have they not, by their very profession, set aside all unnecessary business? Do they not employ a great deal of time in 'prayer and meditation'? What she is saying in the first mansion cannot apply to them. 'Don't be too sure', says Teresa. It's the heart, the inner attitude that matters and this can remain unchanged in spite of these renunciations and these spiritual practices. It is illusion to imagine that simply by withdrawing physically from 'the world and its corruption' we have escaped it. This world is within our own hearts. In a multitude of ways we can reveal we are still ambitious, self-seeking, thoroughly worldly. We may lack the opportunities for gross manifestations of these vices but this can be the more dangerous. Gross manifestations shock us if only because we are ashamed of ourselves, whereas we can commit countless sins and give them scarcely a thought. If we wanted to see them we would, but easily we decline to see them. True prayer brings them to light. Priests, religious and others consciously professing a spiritual life, can be greedy, jealous, sensitive of

18

their rights, worried about their dignity, busybodies, self-important, critical, untruthful snobs – all pure worldliness, the gratification of self not love of God and neighbour. Teresa again insists on the need for self-knowledge. Presumably she found it was missing where it should most be found. We have to be honest with ourselves and often and often accept to bite the dust, but the best way to acquire self-knowledge is not by endless poking into ourselves, trying to turn over this stone and then that to see what reptiles lurk beneath, but by looking constantly at Jesus Christ our Lord. Likewise we need the help of others, those who have greater insight than ourselves and a higher standard, especially those who live with us, who see us in action. Under cover of spirituality we can be terribly self-willed, pursuing the path we have chosen for ourselves, manipulating those with authority over us or to whom we have given a measure of authority, so that they sanction our wishes and provide the spiritual security of 'God's will'. He may be calling us to toil in his vineyard, bearing the burden and heat of the day while we insist that we are called to a more austere form of life, a life of 'deeper prayer'. On the other hand, it may be his will for us that we live the contemplative way of life and we evade the renunciations and responsibilities of this vocation by activity, encouraging a clientele which flatters our pride and provides continual diversion. Pursuing our own will, far from drawing closer to God as we imagine, we are moving away from him. How easily too, our inflated ideas of our spiritual state inspire us with contempt for others, for those not called to so 'high' a vocation as ourselves. We pass judgment – perhaps condescendingly kind – on the lapsed or those who, in our opinion, have lapsed, who do not conform with our ideas of holiness. This is pure worldliness.

Let us remind ourselves over and over again that holiness has to do with very ordinary things: truthfulness, courtesy, kindness, gentleness, consideration for others, contentment with our lot, honesty and courage in the face of life, reliability, dutifulness. Intent, as we think, on the higher reaches of spirituality, we can overlook the warp and woof of holiness.

Second Mansion

Teresa's warmest sympathies are involved with those who have entered the second mansions. She has in mind very real people – she knows them well, and presumably her own daughters are, generally speaking, among them. It is no use looking for a clear cut description of this state or those in it, it is too much like real life for that. What we can always do, and this is true of each mansion, is to discern those elements which are distinctive and proper to it. Teresa gives them straight away. Those are in the second mansions who have made an earnest start in giving themselves to God, and this, for her, writing as she is for a Catholic milieu, always presupposes a resolution to pray. Though still very weak, the resolution is there and it is earnestness which distinguishes this mansion from the previous one. The grace which is offered and accepted is commonly known as 'conversion' and Teresa seems to have in mind a marked one, perhaps her own. But we have to remember that many people can never point to particular moment when they came to a clear realisation of the shoddiness of their lives and the paramount need to do something about it. This is often the case with lay people, who have not been called to change their state of life, and they can easily feel that they have been 'left out', that something has been denied them which has been given to others, who are very special to God. Lacking any marked experience they can settle for a mediocre life it is true, yet some, unknown to themselves, are far from mediocre. Imperceptibly, they have become more faithful as the years have passed, more charitable, more truthful, more reliable. What they would call 'saying their prayers' has become a much deeper reality, though the outward form may have changed little, and the same goes for their participation in the Mass. One of the principle objectives of this commentary is precisely to dissipate the almost universally held conviction – and it *is* almost universal in practice though there are those who would verbally subscribe to the opposite, – that the sensible grace is the *real* thing and the non-sensible a second rate product. It seems to me that it is often those whose lives bear none of these supposedly authenticating experiences who are the closest to God. There is enormous danger of secret vanity and illusion in spiritual impressions. Alas though, because of the ingrained conviction to the contrary, people feel discouraged and 'left out' and therefore don't pray, don't surrender to God as he wants each of them to do. I hope this book of mine convinces them of their own call, as unique and beautiful as they can possibly imagine.

The other distinguishing characteristic of those in this mansion is the nature of their prayer. Prayer must be understood as a state of being, not just a particular activity. Our prayer is precisely our relation to God, what we are face to face with him. It is our stage of growth as a person. God is always calling, always summoning us into being; he is never inactive, never uninvolved, but the capacity to receive him is of varying depths. In this mansion there is relatively little; it will increase by active love. It isn't really true to say we pray because we have a soul or are a soul, we pray in order to become a soul. The second mansions represent a state of being where there is no spiritual 'depth' for God to touch directly; he can only communicate with the reality that is there, and this is material. Teresa points out that God's appeals come through the body, through the senses, by means of good conversations, sermons, books, good thoughts and feelings, sickness, trials and other events of life. She is careful to note that there *is* a different mode of divine communication but this is for later on. Thus, the second mansion is distinguished from later ones by the fact that God can communicate himself only *indirectly*; but, and this is what matters, he is bent on bringing us on, he wants our growth, he wants the seed to germinate beneath the soil, to put down its tap root, to feed on the salts, until it is ready for its contact with the sun, then it can burst through the dark earth at the call of the sun to receive its life-giving rays. This stage cannot be skipped.

21

It is not a question of God withholding his graces from some and giving them to others so that some are bathed in sunshine from the start. God is always giving himself but we must grow to receive him. Were the germinating seed exposed too soon to the rays of the sun it would be destroyed. What merely *feels* like sunshine need have nothing to do with the sunshine spoken of here, which is the only one that matters.

Teresa knows that this is an important stage and everything depends on generosity, the determination to go forward no matter what the difficulties, and she puts forth her energy to persuade and encourage. We hear her in the *Way of Perfection*:

> As I say it is most important – all important indeed – that they should begin well by making an earnest and most determined resolve not to halt until they reach the goal or die on the road or have not heart to confront the trials which they meet, whether the very world dissolves around them.

How few of us resolve like this. When we read such words doesn't our concern for the service of our Lord seem like spineless dilettantism?

Because we have grown, we see and understand more, our obligations are clearer and yet, alas, we experience that the good we ought to do, we do not do. What had seemed innocent is now seen as sinful. This is very painful. Teresa always sees this conflict and pain in a personal context: our Lord is calling in love and we are unable to respond fully. The labour of prayer is hard and the labour of prayer in life is hard, for they are one thing. We must wage war on ourselves, on our self-love, and self-indulgence. We have to strive for detachment from everything that is not God and, as stimulus is often absent, it is very hard and calls for real generosity. This is where the parting of the way starts: one to a life wholly for God, or one to mediocrity. Every possible means must be taken to strengthen our resolve, to maintain a relentless determination to persevere for in no other way can we answer God's call as we should.

> Take my advice and do not tarry on the way, but strive like strong men until you die in the attempt . . . If you always

peruse this determination to die rather than fail to reach the end of the road, the Lord may bring you through this life with a certain degree of thirst, but in the life which never ends he will give you a great abundance with no fear of it ever failing you. (*Way of Perfection*, xx)

We are called to love God above all things with our whole heart and soul and mind. Love is not a mood of delight or contentment, it is not a warm feeling, it is not an inner glow. Love is choosing. I have to choose to love God when my conscious being feels no attraction save for what is here and now desirable. My mind has to supply strong motives for choosing God and his will in concrete instances. Here, I would say, lies our chief weakness. Not sufficient importance is attached to the work the mind must do to set before the heart the motives for choosing what is not immediately and sensibly appealing. This deficiency implies a lack of seriousness and an unwillingness to take trouble. Anyone who really wants God will ceaselessly be thinking of what to do in order to go forward. They will have an eagerness to learn and willingly go to endless trouble. There is a tendency to think that good desires and strong motives will be infused; that if we remain quietly before the Lord in prayer, they will be born in on us; that, when we are tempted and troubled we have only to go before the Lord and we will be changed. It seems to me that a very, very important point is being underplayed. Understandably there has been a reaction to a mistaken form of meditation which put the whole weight on the intellect as though it were a matter of achieving suitable thoughts of God, intellectual and emotional impressions. What matters is 'loving much'. Loving means choosing. I'm not 'loving much' because I am in thoughtless prayer and with a feeling of love. I am loving much when I pour out my life over the feet of Jesus in his brethren. I have to bring before my mind all sorts of reasons for doing this. I have to get to know God and this will mean getting to know Jesus. But there are other powerful incentives that perhaps have to precede the loving preoccupation with Jesus: consideration of the brevity of our life-span, its mysteriousness, what it is for, its gravity and the

23

appalling danger of wasting it. All day long, if we take the trouble, we can glean in the field of our lives, abundant motives for surrendering ourselves to life's whole meaning – God. We must always have in hand the sword of the spirit which is the word of God with which to combat the temptations to give up the struggle, to fall back into worldliness, to sin in one way or another. We have to be ready with the motives for resisting. By and large this seems badly neglected. We fall, we are sorry, but we don't take any special precaution against the future. What we should do, if we are in earnest, is to have our sword ready in hand for the attack – some thought, some word of remembrance of Jesus which, through deep pondering, has become powerful for us.

There is no question of saying that we must spend our time of prayer in thinking, but only in ensuring we are really directed to God, really choosing him; and at this stage we can do this only insofar as our minds furnish the motives. Needless to say, in all this God's grace is active. He is helping us, yet will never do for us what we can do for ourselves. To insist again, it isn't a case of his refusing to do for us what we can do for ourselves, but that it is this human activity of choosing – a joint operation of mind and heart – which gives growth so that God can do for us what we can't do for ourselves.

Teresa tells us that she will be brief on the second mansion as she has written about it a great deal elsewhere. To my mind, some of her most attractive writing revolves around it. Take for instance, the three beautiful chapters in the *Life* where she describes those who 'are beginning to be servants of love – for this, I think, is what we became when we resolve to follow in this way of prayer him who so greatly loved us.' This commentary must be confined to the *Interior Castle* and the temptation to disgress into Teresa's other writings must be resisted. Chapters xi–xii of the *Life* give most helpful teaching on the early stages of prayer. The same must be said of the *Way of Perfection*, from the beginning to xxix. Teresa's primary concern in the *Interior Castle* is to treat of what she calls 'supernatural' prayer, but she can only do this successfully by beginning 'right from the beginning'. All the same, she doesn't want to delay on that which is common knowledge, what has been treated of by many, many others. We can be sure, therefore, that what she actually notes here will be those things that stand out for her as supremely important.

In the *Life* she has exhorted the weary gardener, toiling away with his buckets at the well, to be content, not to complain of the hardship but to seek to please the gardener, not himself. She underlines this same singlemindedness in the *Interior Castle*. We must not think of such things as 'spiritual favours'. We must resolve to seek God and not ourselves. It is this which makes perseverance really hard and is the test of true love – to go on with no satisfying feedback, with nothing, seemingly, for ourselves. Again, the parting of the ways – to holiness or to mediocrity. This is what it means to embrace the cross – and how much we need to look at Jesus, the Beloved, and his obedience unto death if we are to be generous. Nothing happens, nothing reassuring, nothing to say that God hears my prayers. And yet every certainty, every assurance in faith. Unless we make up our minds from the start to embrace the cross we shall never get anywhere. Prayer is not self-culture but self-forgetfulness in God. It will be well to quote Teresa's own strong affirmation of what prayer at this stage really is all about: 'to labour to be resolute and prepare with all possible diligence to bring his will into conformity with the will of God ... this comprises the very greatest perfection which can be attained on the spiritual road. The more perfectly a person practises it, the more he will receive of the Lord and the greater progress he will make along this road; do not think we have to use strange jargon or dabble in things of which we have no knowledge of understanding; our entire welfare is to be found in what I have described.'

Once again, it is hard going. Teresa is specially concerned because the commonly accepted standard of goodness is low. We are all of us bitten by those poisonous vipers but don't realise it. We contaminate one another and don't strive for healing because we don't realise we are diseased. Once again a strong argument why we must think for ourselves, deeply, constantly so as not to be conditioned by the standards around us. She has spelt out in the *Way* how pernicious are the bad habits

25

connected with sensitiveness to honour, to one's rights and so forth and how they become acceptable behaviour even for the devout. Until we have made a firm stand against these false values we can never hope to grow.

This second mansion is more like a railway station than a chamber of a castle made for living in. A railway station is for arrivals and departures. Everything is astir, charged with tensions of farewell, brave dashes to board the train which will take one far away from what one loves and clings to; second thoughts .... delays ... grief, fear, repugnance and also happy, mysterious anticipation. Let us not forget it. Where God is there is happiness; God never asks us for useless sacrifice. God wants us to grow and growth means increase in capacity for happiness. If we have to forego childish enjoyments we soon learn to appreciate the riches of maturer life.

Third Mansion

God is love, an intensity of desire to bring us to the fulness of being which is our perfect happiness. This purpose of God never wavers, it is concentrated, white-hot on each individual. If then, growth does not happen or happens very inadequately we have to look for the cause in us, not in our Father. If someone were to persevere with the determination and generosity Teresa has urged, without doubt, as inevitably as spring follows winter, there would be growth such as would enable us to bear, in no matter how small a degree, the direct contact with God which he is longing to effect. Without any doubt whatever he would communicate himself. Yet actual experience reveals that this does not always happen. We must look for the reason within ourselves.

There was a time when I took it for granted that the third mansion represented a first goal, a modest one indeed, but a goal none the less. Now, I see it as a stopping place, somewhere that should not be; we have settled down and made our home in the railway station. We should travel non-stop – and we would, were we generous – to that blessed, all desirable rendezvous with the Lord to which he is calling us. 'O why,' cries impassioned Teresa,

when a soul has resolved to love thee and by forsaking everything does all in its power towards that end, so that it may better employ itself in the love of the God, hast thou been pleased that it should not at once have the joy of ascending to the perfection of this perfect love? But I am wrong: I should have made my complaint by asking why we ourselves have no desire to ascend, for it is we alone who are at fault in not at once enjoying so great a dignity! . . . so niggardly and so slow are we in giving ourselves wholly to God that we do not

27

prepare as we should to receive the precious thing which it is His Majesty's will we should enjoy only at a price. (*Life*, XI.)

Though the third mansion is a state that ought not to be, Teresa has to admit that it seems the normal state of most good people and so she gives it her attention, diagnosing its weakness.

She begins by praising those who have reached this stage: the bewildering and deceptive thing about it, is that there seems much to praise. If we meet people who have overcome their bad habits, who live carefully ordered lives materially and spiritually, whom nothing would induce to sin, who love doing penance, spend hours in recollection, who use their time well, practice works of charity towards their neighbour and are very careful in their speech and dress, would we think them not only admirable but saintly? Aren't we inclined to say 'so and so is a perfect saint'? Teresa doesn't think so and her exposé of this state is one of her most fruitful contributions to the understanding of what growth in the spirit really is. It is because this state seems so good and exemplary, that it is a stumbling block to true holiness. Too often this third mansion in real life is taken to be the summit of the spiritual life: it tends to satisfy us and those around us yet it is far from what Christianity is all about. Teresa is happier and more at ease writing of the second mansion. It is truer, healthier. There we are consciously struggling with sin that humiliates us. In the first mansion, because there is no light, we can overestimate ourselves, but in the second we have become exposed to the light a little and this inevitably is humiliating. If this first gleam of self-knowledge and humility are absent then we are not in the second mansion.

Teresa has already warned us of the need for welcoming, never shirking, the painful awareness of our sinful self. But alas, this is a hard thing for us humans because we don't know God, we don't really believe in his unconditional love no matter how much we say that we do. To stand before him as we are in our naked shame, and not to run away and hide, or deck ourselves in our fine thinking to conceal our poor reality, we have to believe in his love. We reduce God to our own likeness, and this in great measure, I think, because we have not taken the trouble to go to the source, to find out for ourselves in the scriptures, and above all in Jesus, what he is really like. We prefer to live with our preconceived notions or with what others communicate to us, and the result is a caricature of God which at one and the same time gives us comfort because, having him in our image, we can cope with him; and despair because, again seeing him in our own image, we feel he hates us for our ugliness. Therefore we can't afford to be ugly, we have to hide it from ourselves and so we bury it all deep down; we bury the gnawing doubts and fears, and manage to achieve a state of relative self-satisfaction. Our seemingly excellent behaviour gives support to this self-satisfaction. It is of enormous consequence to us that we behave well, that our thoughts, desires, actions are those of a 'spiritual person'. Tremendous inner energies are at work to produce this 'perfection' which has in fact nothing to do with true growth.

What has happened is that the roots of our basic selfishness have been left untouched. This selfishness takes ever more subtle forms which, because they are subtle, do not cause the humiliation and shame of grosser manifestations. This is the danger Teresa is alive to. More than once she warns her own nuns that they must watch that they do not fall into the error of thinking themselves better than they are because occasions for gross faults are removed. What happens so often is, that after the first impulse of grace which drove us to generosity, we slacken off and fall back into bad habits, but because their manifestations are slight, we don't tackle them relentlessly, we let them be. By and large they don't spoil the outward facade – yet though the cracks seem tiny the damage is great. Teresa warns: don't be so sure. Fear! fear yourselves! fear the Lord!, not in the sense of fearing someone like our mean selves ready to find fault and punish, but as the all holy, whose standards utterly surpass our own. Fear of the Lord means we have a keen realisation that only his judgements matter. What I am in his eyes, that I am and no other. My actions have the value he sees them to have and no other. What we are in our own eyes, what we are in the eyes of others is of no consequence yet how easily we forget this in practice. Jesus begs us to watch this, to make sure that our hearts are fixed on our Father in heaven, that all the time we are looking into his face as we do our works of fasting, alms deeds and prayer. Such a pure-hearted gaze would eliminate all complacency, all casualness and we would know the psalmist's cry 'no one is just in your eyes'.

Virtue is often more apparent than real, the roots of sin remain strong and tenacious but the foliage, for the present, looks alright. We are deceived because we want to be, being more concerned with our own spiritual image than in becoming all God's. We have a deep secret satisfaction with ourselves; we do really feel we are advanced though would never say so even to ourselves. We practise the externals of humility and this means humble acknowledgements about self, our faults, our lack of progress; Oh yes, we are poor sinners! But we don't really think so. Teresa helps us to recognise our illusion and if we study the examples she gives with great care, we can learn a lot.

Here is someone who automatically puts everything in an edifying context. A spade is never a spade. He doesn't want to recognise his covetousness and lack of detachment, and his self-esteem finds ways of explaining to himself why he feels and acts as he does. No one can offer advice because he knows all there is to know, after all, he is an adept at the spiritual life, he can give good advice to others. The aches, pains, humiliations which flow from the simple realities of human life or from his own self-esteem become 'suffering for God'. Everything, everything becomes perverted and made a sop for self-esteem. He just can't take the lessons Our Lord is trying to teach. Teresa turns on her own daughters lest they should be complacently thinking this example has nothing to do with them after all, they don't have property to lose, they have no worldly ambitions. She points out how the same vices are in them. Watch those seemingly trifling incidents, a slight that arouses my indignation, note how I stand on my dignity, claim my little rights, how I think I have a *right* to feel wronged because I have been passed over, removed from a particular job, left aside, not appreciated as I think I ought to be. If we were to make a fuss in public then we would feel shamed because our weakness would be revealed, but when the wrong reactions are concealed by pieties, grace of manner, subtleties, then we feel no shame whatever. We don't think they matter. Teresa is quite obsessed, we shall find, by this basic concern for our 'honour'. She sees it as *the* problem – an underlying lack of humility. She worries because it is so common as to be accepted as normal and it is not seen as the vice it is. It is merely 'human', smiled at in others, compatible with holiness because we accept it in ourselves. Few realize its importance. The whole law of growth is a movement away from self. If the growing point of a seed were to remain folded up within the acorn it would come to nothing. It has to uncurl, push itself out, up and away. We can only become by leaving ourselves. Here we are choosing to stay in self. We have tidied self up, made it respectable and possible to live with and now we settle down, not prepared for that total forsaking of self, that total love of neighbour which is true growth in the spirit. We are clinging to the world of 'flesh and blood' as Paul would say, deciding to stay in the womb. Deciding? Yes, a choice is being made. It is we who are choosing to shut out the call, the creative call to a wholly new life, a new way of being, the way of 'spirit'.

Teresa has another criticism: our penances are as well-ordered as our lives. She satirises our calculating service of God. What does she mean by penances? In her day penances, that is voluntarily accepted forms of self-denial such as fasting, wearing hair shirts, vigils, were the accepted sign of generosity, of the desire to give all, to go beyond what was asked. Teresa is pointing out that we lack wholeheartedness. We say we want God, perhaps we feel we do, but where is the proof, where that stretching of self, where that total pre-occupation, that stopping at nothing which is characteristic of real desire? No, we are carefully protecting ourselves, prepared to give so much but no more, ensuring that we are not aware that there is a more to give. When what is asked is painful to our self-esteem, when it bites then, no, we shouldn't be asked that, anything else, but not that. . . . We are afraid of what the service of God might bring, we are afraid of being bored, of being tired, of losing face, of having nothing for ourselves . . . We will live for God so long as it pays, so long as we get something out of it, but when there is nothing at all for self then we refuse to see that there is anything more to do.

How can we describe generosity? There is no pattern for it. We can't imitate anyone else's expressions of generosity. The form it takes for one may not be the form it takes in another. What we have to do is earnestly beg for the grace to be generous, for the light to see what is wanted of us, not in general but at every particular moment. There is literally not a moment when I am not being given a choice between God and myself. True generosity is always alert, always 'there', eagerly looking for the Lord, ready to throw its arms around him whatever his guise. It doesn't drift through life, sticking to patterned behaviour and missing these living encounters in my neighbour, in the duty of the moment, in this little humiliation, in this physical pain, in this disappointment, in this pleasure and joy. We are not to wait for our glorious hour, the hour of testing when we shall be called upon to show our generosity. That hour may never come and if it does, we shall respond in the same measure as we respond to him in his humble guise hour by hour. It is not a case of seeking suffering but a determination to disregard self, to accept life as it is, to be wholly at the service of others, faithful to our obligations great and small no matter how tedious, unromantic, unrewarding; willing to shoulder burdens that may seem too heavy if we are called upon to do so; disdaining to consider whether we are feeling happy or sad, consoled or afflicted. This wholeheartedness is the way to happiness, whereas the careful, calculating life is fatiguing, full of stumbling blocks and fears. We must pray for and work for an ardent love which overcomes reason.

Teresa has already counselled us to put out of our minds any desire for 'favours' in prayer. For the moment let us substitute 'consolations'. To engage in prayer in order to attain these is a false position from the start. Such an activity is not prayer, it is self-culture. But even though we do not blatantly act in so mercenary a way, still, we expect to receive consolations and when we don't, feel disgruntled, feel we have been let down; after all, we have deserved them. We have lived, long, long years serving God, we have done all that we should, why haven't they come? Why do I feel so dry and empty? People well-instructed in the spiritual life are not likely, I think, to seek striking 'favours' but there will be few of us who don't seek more modest varieties. We want the certainty that we are advanced and not among the ranks of beginners. We run over in our minds the hardships we have undergone, the sacrifices we have made, the good works we have slogged at . . . surely I deserve to be advanced, don't I? We haven't grasped that all is pure gift, that I can't earn advancement, that I can't, by doing this, that, or the other, demand of God, 'now do your part!' No amount of suffering or sacrifice can draw God down to us. Teresa reminds us of what our Lord himself has taught, that he can give himself only to the humble, only to those who know they have earned nothing, only those who treat God as a Father who, they are certain, seeks their best interests, not a master bound in justice to pay his servants what they have earned. He will send us over and over again occasions, probably quite small ones, for seeing and acknowledging how unworthy we are. Aren't there times when all of us feel deeply humbled, our meanness, our ugliness painfully revealed and perhaps for a short time we know the happiness of humble acceptance and truth. Alas, we quickly fall back into our blindness and push away the painful memory, or artificially neutralise the shame by extravagant, edifying acts of humility which supply the compensating boost to our fading image. Until we are prepared to grow beyond this crippling, life-killing shell of self-interest we can never be ready for God. We are not there for him to come to, we are strangled at birth.

As people who live well-ordered lives, who are initiated into the charmed circles of the spiritual life and know all about it we are readily critical of others. We have clear ideas of how devout people should act and if they don't conform to these they are open to censure. We could probably learn a lot from those we are criticising, perhaps they have far greater knowledge and love of God than we have and it is this which gives them freedom to forget themselves. When we have gained a little experience, because we are still so blind we fancy ourselves far wiser and more spiritual than we are and feel are in a position to instruct and admonish one another. It were better if we looked only at our selves. True, all of us need help, support, enlightenment from one another and must be ready to seek for and accept this help, but in order to help we have first to love. If we love someone and desire their true good then we can probably give them useful advice according to the light we have. Because we love them it will be humble and sincere. Until we are sure we really love others if is not safe to look at their faults or pass any judgement whatever. Only love can see clearly. Teresa would like us to have someone more advanced than ourselves, to give us light and urge us on. The trouble is that as often as not this is the person we keep clear of and we fly for refuge to those of our own standards where we can feel comfortable and at home. After all, it pays us to console one another. The disturbing interloper must be silenced. All this is sheer proof of our cowardice and lack of sincerity. If we really wanted God we would be eager to be told, eager to find someone who knows him and can direct us to him. The desire to shelter, to be protected from the demands of God makes us self-willed, self-determined. Teresa begs us to accept to be submissive and obedient, to let go the controls of our own life. We don't need to be in a religious order to make this surrender of will. Countless opportunities are there for us all. Once we grasp that our sinful self-seeking is the mortal enemy of God we will be eager for such occasions. Life is full of them if only we are on the lookout.

This is an unhappy state. We are labouring under a great load of earth which hampers our movements and takes away the joy of life. Yet it is self-chosen. God never leaves us alone and is always trying to liberate us but the tragedy is that as the years go by, as time and time again we refuse this liberation, we grow more and more fixed in our ways. Perhaps the sense of oppression and weariness is at last stifled and we are so complacent that we are oblivious of the fact that we are utterly unspiritual, are totally blind to our own reality in a cocoon of illusory peace. The Lord is helpless. Perhaps the last illness, perhaps death provide the shattering experience which will bring the healing revelation. But it is tragedy all the same for the love of God is

34

beating round us, Spirit and Fire, storming our ramparts to effect an entrance; the kingdom is seeking a weak point for invasion but no, the impregnable fortress remains unconquered.

Fourth Mansion, Part I

It is when we come to the fourth mansion that our problems start. Here, says Teresa, we 'begin to touch the supernatural'. 'Supernatural prayer,' 'infused contemplation', these for Teresa, mean the same thing, and we are going to add 'mystical contemplation' as synonymous, also. This entity, whatever it is, is the theme of all her writings. The ascetic path she marks out, whether in the *Life*, the *Way of Perfection* or the first three mansions of the *Interior Castle*; the insistence on the hard work needed to detach ourselves from ourselves; the practice of the virtues and fidelity to prayer, all are orientated to the reception of infused contemplation. She sees it as something utterly precious, a pearl beyond price, to be desired with ardour and laboured for with everything we have, not because we can actually acquire it, for we cannot, but its bestowal demands a generous preparation on our part. What is said here of St Teresa can be said equally of St John of the Cross. This talk of infused contemplation did not originate with them, they took over without question a terminology already well established.

What then is this 'infused contemplation'? Is it something only a very few priviliged persons may aspire to or is it something that is the very stuff of human fulfilment? A cloud of bewildering misconceptions envelops and obscures the subject; it has hung over it for centuries. This chapter is an attempt at explanation, if indeed one can speak of explaining what is of God himself. I hope two things will strike the reader as we progress: firstly that what is said here is wholly in line with tradition; secondly, that, within that tradition, a bold break is being made, a break with age-long, popular, even 'professional' interpretation of the tradition. Unless both are seen, then either I have not expressed myself well or am being misread.

Let me begin this discussion with personal reminiscences which, I imagine, will ring bells in many a mind. There were not many books in our small library when I entered Carmel many years ago, but what few there were immediately put one in a mysterious, alien world. Here was a strange vocabulary that bore no relation, it seemed, to the rest of life. It was like a spiritual code. A rapid glance down the index of what is a recognised classic of the mystical tradition, *The Graces of Interior Prayer*, by A. Poulain, SJ, published in the early years of this century, will give an idea of what I mean: Mystical graces or touches; Prayer of Quiet, Prayer of full union; Five spiritual senses; The soul attains to God by a spiritual touch; Physiological features of ecstasy; On the ligature during the prayer of full union, etc. and this is to confine ourselves to the less esoteric topics. What does it all mean? What relation has it to real life? Reading through the gospels, redolent with everything that is real in life, where does this strange jargon fit in? These were the questions I asked myself. Clearly some people saw sense in it, saw a connection with the gospels, with real life, even if I could not. Worse, reading what Teresa has to say of her own states of prayer, states such as Poulain and many others would consider utterly sublime, as most intimate communications of God, around which treatise after treatise has been written throughout the centuries, far from being impressed, I found myself put off. It seemed to cheapen God and I found myself hoping it wasn't God! What I see I was really saying, is 'it can't be God'. That conviction, timidly held by sheer intuition and commonsense so long ago, I now maintain unwaveringly. For many, many years, I have wrestled with the problem, seeking intellectual clarity. No author has helped me save John of the Cross, but it was a long time before I could understand him comprehensively. All others, it seemed to me, assume the identity of what Teresa *describes* of her state of prayer, that is, what she *felt* of that state, with the *state itself*; what, in her case, *accompanied* the mystical state with the *reality itself*. My conviction is that anything that can be described, given an account of, simply cannot be the mystical encounter in itself. Why is this so? Because the mystical encounter is precisely a *direct* encounter with God himself. Both Teresa and John are quite sure of this; it is the fundamental statement they make about it: this water flows 'direct from the source'; 'God has drawn near', he is 'very close'; and for John of the Cross it is 'an inflowing of God into the soul'. They see earlier forms of prayer as 'indirect'; God speaking, communicating, etc. through 'natural' channels, in the 'ordinary' way. Infused or mystical contemplation is *God in direct contact*; God himself, not a created image of him, and therefore 'supernatural' in regard to the subject; contacting in a way beyond the ordinary faculties, therefore 'supernatural' in its mode, also. This, I am certain no one will dispute. When we insist that this encounter with God himself, must, of its nature, bypass, or transcend our material faculties we are saying that it must be 'secret' – John of the Cross insists on this – 'from the intellect that receives it'.

What then are we looking at when we are shown these marvellous, so-called 'mystical experiences' such as Poulain has in mind? We will confine ourselves to Teresa herself. What are we looking at? She herself loved the images of garden and water. Let us think of her as a garden, a very fertile garden irrigated by a deep underground spring which never fails. Over this garden a beautiful fountain plays and our first impression is that this fountain is the source of the garden's fertility, that this it is that irrigates the soil, and, we have to say, if the garden were conscious, it would think so too! We are mistaken and if we look closely we shall see that what we are looking at is not a real fountain at all, it is a phenomenon arising from the particular district the garden is in, the particular consistency of the soil, and the temperature. Moisture from this well-watered garden is caught up and overhangs it like a fountain playing, and perhaps the soft, moist canopy above does refresh the flowers. But certainly it is not the source of the garden's fertility. We are suggesting that, in Teresa's case, there *is* a connection between the underground spring which cannot be seen and that which can be seen, the beautiful pseudo-fountain. In other words, the 'favours' in her case, are an effect of the mystical grace but they are *not* the mystical grace nor in anyway essential to it. They only make the garden more beautiful and interesting to observe.

Now let us visit another garden. A lovely sight! A glorious fountain arcs from one end to the other, breaking up the light, lovely as a rainbow. We are lost in admiration – and so is the garden – but . . . one moment . . . look at the cabbages! Look at the flowers! Where are they? A few withered stalks, we can hardly see them. The ground is parched and barren, there is no underground spring. What has produced this fountain then? There could be lots of explanations, some scientific trick or other, particular minerals in the soil, but what is certain in this case is that it has nothing to do with an underground spring, for clearly the spring isn't there! In some cases, and definitely so in Teresa's case, the mystical grace overflows as it were into the psychic powers. But we can *never* assume that similar experiences must spring from the same mystical source. And we would stress again that, even in the case of such as Teresa, this overflow has little significance compared with the reality of the grace, as the illusory fountain compared with the underground spring. 'By their fruits you shall know them'. But the fruits of genuine mystical contemplation are of a very special quality indeed.

Another illustration of the relationship between the mystical grace and its possible overflow is that between goodness and charm. We all see this, don't we? Some people are richly endowed with that mysterious quality we call charm. What is it? We can't say. Some have it, some do not. But have we noticed now quite ordinary goodness, accompanied by charm, begins to glow? Only too easily the goodness is over estimated; it begins to dazzle us. Too easily we fail to see that it is the charm which is dazzling us. An equal goodness in one devoid of charm would be overlooked. It is probably true that goodness and still more, holiness give a special quality to charm, but in itself it is absolutely distinct from it. Holiness without charm is rarely recognised. On the other hand, you can have fascinating charm and the popularity that goes with it, with very little goodness. Again, it is a question of the quality of the flowers and cabbages, not the beauty of the fountain that matters.

Insisting on this distinction between the mystical encounter

39

itself and the possible effect of this in the psychic powers, is to oppose centuries of high esteem for 'the feeling of the presence of God' to single out perhaps the most modest claim to mystical grace. Yet it is hard to see how any open, intelligent mind could fail to see the inherent contradictions in treatises on mysticism, where this esteem is present. You see them in Teresa's own writings and her inevitable self-questioning which drove her to seek authoritative assurance for what was happening to her, because, deep down, 'something isn't quite right somewhere'. Somewhere, there is a huge question mark. You find it verbalised, for instance, in the disputed question as to whether the call to the mystical life is for all; whether infused contemplation is essential for holiness or whether one can be holy and yet not have received this gift. These questions have absorbed the attention of grave men over the centuries, leading to the formation of different 'schools' of spirituality – one holding one view, another the other. The Carmelite school had to devise a form of prayer called 'active contemplation' to cope with the problem. How simple the answer to all this did we but concentrate on the teaching of the gospels and carefully hold in mind the distinction made above.

See the trouble Poulain runs into when he asks if it is presumption to desire the mystical state:

> If the supernatural states of prayer were merely means of sanctification, graces of sanctity, the question of desiring them would present no difficulty. But they are extraordinary graces, privileges, divine familiarities, bringing with them marvels of condescention on God's part, and elevating the soul to heights that are regarded without exception by ordinary people as sublime. (*The Graces of Interior Prayer.*)

This passage surely epitomises the contradiction running unsolved through the tradition. It comes from the fact that the attention and emphasis are on the human partner in the relationship of prayer. The criterion for assessing a state of prayer is taken to be what the human partner either does or feels. If they are aware of the presence of God, as they would say, if they feel 'held', are absorbed, then we can assume the presence of mystical prayer – this *is* mystical prayer; on the other hand, if there is none of this 'suspension', no feeling of God's presence, then we have to say the prayer is not mystical. But when we think about it, is not this an extraordinary thing to do? Surely the very essence of prayer, even in the early stages, is to be there for the God whose very nature is to give. This is superlatively true in the mystical prayer, for this, par excellence, is 'what God is doing'. How can we possibly think that it is all that important how the human partner comports himself, whether he uses his mind in this way or that, whether his psyche produces this or that, as though God's activity in us is dependant on such things. How can we think that what we feel or don't feel, what we know or don't know is all important. If we have faith, surely we *know* that God gives himself without measure and we won't attempt to gauge the depth of the giving by our totally inadequate plumb lines of sense.

Let us take up the point of sanctity. Poulain is telling us that mystical graces are distinct from 'graces of sanctity'. What is sanctity? Poulain suggests that it is a degree below the 'privileges', the 'divine familiarities' of mystical union. Surely sanctity necessarily implies these, sanctity *is* mystical union. Surely the message of the New Testament is that union with God, divine intimacy, familiarity, unheard of privilege, is what man is for, it is the promise of the Father offered in Jesus and for which he died. We are called to be sons in the Son, heirs of God because co-heirs with Christ, sharing in the divine nature, filled with the fulness of God. If mystical union is not one and the same thing with this promise of the Father totally effected in a human being, redemption completed, then it is something bogus. There can be no higher gift than what the New Testament tells us is the common destiny of man.

W.H. Vanstone in his book *Love's Endeavour, Love's Expense*, has a moving passage on the lavishness of God and the destiny of creation. It is the heart of revelation:

The activity of God must be limitless creativity. It must set no interior limit to its own self-giving. It must ever seek to enlarge the capacity to receive of the 'other' to which it gives.

41

The infinity of the universe must be understood, with awe, as the expression or consequence of the limitlessness of the divine self-giving: for the divine aspiration to give must ever enlarge the bounds of that which is to receive. Nothing must be withheld from the self-giving which is creation: no unexpended reserves of divine potentiality: no 'glory of God' or 'majesty of God' which may be compared and contrasted with the glory of the galaxies and the majesty of the universe: no 'power of God' which might over-ride the God-given powers of the universe: no 'eternity of God' which might outlive an 'eternal universe'.... From this self-giving nothing is held back: nothing remains in God unexpended.

This Self-squanderer does not carefully weigh out his gifts, offering 'divine familiarities' to a few, withholding them from others; he is not overflowing generosity to some, miserliness with others. He is always giving himself insofar as he *can* be received and he is always trying to enlarge the capacity so that he can give himself more fully. Without any doubt there are some and perhaps only the few, who have entered in this life into profoundest intimacy with God, but this intimacy, this state of mystical union simply cannot be attested by such psychic experiences as Poulain speaks of. Jesus himself gives us the criterion. It is loving 'as I have loved you', keeping his commandments as he keeps his Father's, it is living as he did in total surrender. This conformity with Jesus, this total surrender, is impossible to human effort, a divine gift is needed, an infusion of divine energy, the Spirit of Jesus himself, the Promise of the Father. This is precisely what we mean by mystical, infused contemplation.

If we strip to the bone what both Teresa and John have to say of the gift, we find: it is *pure gift*, something we can never achieve for ourselves...! however much we may practise meditation, however much we do violence to ourselves, and however many tears we shed, we cannot produce this water in those ways....' It is something entirely *new*. It is not a deepening of what has gone before, an increasing expertise, not a continuation, but a break.

It is, as already said, a *direct* encounter with God.

It *purifies* and *transforms*.

Although it can never be achieved it calls for a *generous preparation*.

Do we not see that this is just what the new Testament is telling us of the Father's promise: the 'kingdom of God' in the synoptists, 'eternal life' in John, living with the life of Christ in Paul. When, in the *Way of Perfection*, Teresa begins to speak of the first mystical graces, significantly it is in the context of the Pater Noster, 'Thy kingdom come,' 'He begins to give us his kingdom on earth!' (*Way*, xxxl)

The theme of the kingdom, is for Jesus, the song of his heart; it is springtime breaking in on a wintered world, bringing the world into flower; he laid down his life to bring it in. His parables reveal the secrets of the kingdom to those who can really hear what he is saying, to the little ones of humble heart. Sometimes the kingdom is seen as something coming upon us, or as something within us. Listening to the parables we can be diverted, I think, from their deepest meaning by fixing our attention on what might seem a collective aspect of the kingdom: the seed sown so humbly in Israel will have a world-wide impact for instance; but does this really make sense? God does not give himself to collectives but only to individuals. If the kingdom does impregnate the world of men it can only be because individual hearts have received it. Only individuals, transformed into love are the presence of Love in the world. The leaven is offered to an individual heart to be its transforming principle, offered to be accepted or rejected. If received, there is no end to its inherent power to transform. The seed, welcomed in well-prepared soil has a dynamism of its own which will burgeon into a magnificent fruitfulness; if the soil is unwelcoming through its unpreparedness, the seed comes to nothing.

The forgiving love of the Father goes after us as we wander away, escaping from him who is our happiness. Only in his embrace do we find our salvation, only in his embrace are we cleansed of our filth and clothed in beauty. We can accept that embrace of love or we can spend our lives evading it. As W.H. Vanstone points out so movingly, the self-squandering love of God, runs the risk of failure. It is part of the kenosis that the Gift, which is of course, himself, is out of his hands – it can be scorned. The triumph or tragedy of love rests with us. There are parables that reveal our own hearts to us – part of us which does accept love but at the same time part of us that rejects it: the drag net, the field of wheat and tares. Offered to all without exception, there are few that surrender wholly to it, some more, some less, some hardly at all. Truly we can substitute for the 'kingdom', the strange, unlovely terms, infused contemplation or mystical contemplation. How I hate using them; each time I feel a revulsion but must do so if I am to succeed in what I long to do, wipe the slate clean of all images so that everyone can know that there is not a mysterious realm of spiritual reality from which they are debarred. If they wish, they too can be filled with all the fullness of God, 'heights', says Poulain, (and how many with him!) 'regarded by ordinary people as sublime', and, by inference, not for them. The tragedy of it! This is the work of the Adversary from the start. What is the result? An indolence or apathy that seems justified . . . 'such things are not for us'. Fixing our attention on an illusory fountain, mistaking it for the 'fountain of living water' of which Jesus speaks, we have turned away. Yet, if *you* ask of him, he will give *you* living water, says Jesus.

Is not the whole theme of the gospel of John that of something wholly new breaking into the world of men, something divine, something from heaven, a direct encounter with God such as has not been before, and which man, of himself, can never attain or dream of? It is offered freely to all – Jesus cries aloud in the stress of his desire to give – a pure gift. It can never be forced on us, it must be accepted simply because it is the gift of love. Accepted, it purifies and transforms the water of our humanity into the wine of God. It brings into being a wholly new way of God's being with his people, a dwelling in their inmost hearts where he is worshipped in spirit and in truth, in temples which he himself must create. It is an unfailing spring of life-giving water replacing the stagnant pool of man's sinful existence, set in his inmost heart continually renewing the life which is the only true life of man, the life of God himself. It is divine bread, nourishing him and making him live by God, transforming him into God, enabling him to live with an incorruptible life which the body itself is to share and so death will have no meaning. By this new thing men become sons of God. To accept Jesus Christ means accepting his death, entering into it with him: this is the only gate by which this wholly new thing can invade. The cross, surrender to death in order to be created anew, to be born again of the holy Spirit – these awesome thoughts must be present always when we think of mystical union.

There is nothing whatever in the new testament to suggest that this holy gift, the kingdom, eternal life here and now, hits the headlines, compelling assent. Quite the contrary. Jesus suggests its hidden character, lost as it is in the ordinary texture of life. The seed is growing but the farmer does not see it; it grows silently, hiddenly, attracting no attention. His own life among us was just like that and he was scorned and rejected because it was just like that. He repelled the demands for signs and wonders to prove the presence of divine activity. The sign of the outpouring love of God, to be received by all who wish, is the surrender of Jesus on the cross. This is the most divine, the supreme act of creation, the summit of being, and yet, what struck the senses? The tumultuous wind of Pentecost, shaking the foundations of the world, the tongues of fire are only pic-torial images of the hidden activity of God, the promise of the Father which indeed shakes our world to its foundations and fills us with the fire of love.

To press home the point still further, read what the scripture scholar, C.H. Dodd has to say of the 'mutual indwelling' in the last discourse of the gospel of John. It involves 'the most intimate union possible between God and man, a real community of being, a sharing of life . . . it is a dynamic incursion of divine energy through which man may speak and do the words and works of God.' A perfect description of infused contemplation according to Teresa and John of the Cross. Dodd goes on to ask if John the evangelist can properly be called a mystic and considers various uses of the term:

Cosmic emotion is not very common and it is possible for the philosopher to interpret it as unity with 'God' in a pantheistic sense, and so to give colour to what is a theory of the universe. It is possible to interpret certain abnormal psychical states as 'possession' by the divine Spirit. But in neither case have we evidence that union with a personal God is attained. For the only kind of personal union, I repeat, with which we are acquainted, is love. John says that this is in truth the kind of union with God given in the Christian religion . . . it is essentially supernatural and not of this world, and yet plants its feet firmly in this world bearing the fruit of self-sacrificing love for the neighbour. It is not cause but effect of the outpouring love of God.

Dodd concludes: 'Whether this should be called "mysticism" I do not know.' Both Teresa and John of the Cross would answer emphatically, 'that is just what it is!'

The term 'mystical' is by no means confined to Christianity, as well we know. It is one of the words Christianity took over from the cultured world. The word suggests awareness of mysteries, an experience of transcendence, exaltation, a vision through and beyond what immediately strikes the senses, a passing glimpse of an unseesn world. When Christians, in their religious acts, felt something of this – after all, it is a human phenomenon and Christians are human – they naturally fell back on an accepted word. It is this range of experience, commonly dubbed 'mystical' that we need to look at, for by and large, it is precisely this that is confused with the truly mystical, the breakthrough into this world of the divine. The first is a human act and therefore labours under the limitations of 'flesh and blood'; the second is a divine act that transcends these limitations. The confusion of the human psyche with the theological, biblical concept of soul or spirit is common, and is the source of our misunderstandings. Or, even if we do allow the distinction, it is assumed, at least in practice, that the mystical life will inevitably manifest itself in an increase of the psychic powers. This is not so. There are many people who have well-developed psychic awareness. We can conveniently call them 'sensitives'. We find them among all sorts of people in no way religious. What they have is a natural endowment and we can not even say a high endowment. It seems to belong to more primitive peoples. Children have it, as a rule, and it seems to be a stage on the way to full self-awareness. To surrender to psychic impressions would be to become less rather than more human. Generally speaking, psychic powers diminish as self-awareness grows. Now, certain practices associated with the spiritual life, at least unconsciously foster psychic power though this may not be their direct aim: control and silencing of the mind, fasting, lack of sleep. Some practices of Yoga and other philosophies positively induce psychic states as highly desirable states of consciousness. Transpose these same effects into a Christian context of prayer and they are mistaken for true mysticism. We have to admit that generally speaking, those who have left us an account of their journey of prayer, have been among these 'sensitives' and have themselves failed to distinguish between these psychic effects and the mystical grace itself. Teresa was a marked 'sensitive'.

If we have paid attention to modern scientific investigations of the psyche, and it is unreasonable to think we can understand Teresa and other mystics if we have failed to do so, then we shall have come to the conclusion that it is a most mysterious, largely unexplored dimension where almost anything might happen. Were it not scientifically attested one would find quite incredible a great deal of what is claimed: exquisite music creating a feeling of immense happiness and taking away all fear of death; scents that seem to come from no natural source; knowledge of things to come, of what is happening at a great distance; a feeling of being out of the body, looking down at oneself; seeming to be carried to the threshold of death; a paradisal ecstasy. There is no end to what goes on in the world of the psyche. This vast range of experience, often awesome and mysterious, belongs to, is part of our material being. It is not of the 'spirit' in the scriptural, theological sense. It is of 'flesh and blood' as Paul has it that cannot enter the kingdom. It belongs to man as 'animate being', that which we share with the material creation and, in itself, has nothing to do with 'spirit' except in so far as everything material is for the growth of spirit. It is possible to have most lofty 'spiritual experiences', and yet be a mere embryo when it comes to capcity for God. Likewise, such experiences, when in a context of religion and Christian prayer can assume a significance they haven't got. They can operate freely in the earliest stages of the interior life and unless we are clear as to the basic materiality of them, we can be led astray. In those liable to them, who enter the mystic way, they can continue to operate and again can be misinterpreted. Of themselves they are human experiences and, as with everything else, can be used or abused. Understood, used humbly, they can be an incentive and help; God may positively make use of this apparatus when he sees it would help but we must realise that the apparatus is the same in kind as that with which we understand a book, are uplifted and inspired by music, moved by another person: these are all sensible means which God uses to teach and guide us. In themselves they belong to the realm of sense which cannot know spirit directly. The chart may illumine what is written here.

An ambiguity cuts through Teresa's writings on infused contemplation. She is often conscious of it herself but does not know how to solve it. There is no doubt that she confused, indeed identified, in a way John of the Cross never did – he was at pains in his writings to demonstrate to the contrary – what her psychic nature echoed back from a mystical grace, with the grace itself. In her case there *is* something more and this is what we have elsewhere referred to as 'light on'. This is the time to say what we can about it.

The 'light on' experience is not the mystical grace itself, it reveals it. It seems we must say that it is supernatural in the strict sense, that is, that it is of God and not, in itself proper to the human experience of God in this life. That being so it is wiser to leave it in its mystery and concentrate not on its nature but on what it does. What it does is precisely to illuminate the mystical happening which, of itself, is secret. Presumably, it will perform a different function in different people according to God's plan. In Teresa's case, its function seems to have been to reveal her own soul to herself, enabling her to see God's action in her. What we have to grasp is that this gift, puts a person in a class apart – their experience is *fundamentally different from ours*. It is a very rare gift and all of us do well to take for granted we are 'light off' no matter how great our psychic perception and consequent 'spiritual favours'. It is very hard to demonstrate that 'light on' is not identical with what we normally put under the generic term 'spiritual favours'. From reactions to what was written of the subject in *Guidelines for Mystical Prayer*, it is clear that the distinction is not grasped. We must labour it as it is most important. Inevitably the 'light on' person lives in great loneliness once they have begun to realise that others do not share their vision. Teresa, it seems, could never clarify the difference between herself and others; she knew it by effect: her knowledge and certitude contrasted with the ignorance and lack of certitude of others. 'Light on' is the source of the great confidence with which she wrote in an age when there was much to fear and when she had every natural reason for not being sure. It is the source too of her sense of superiority over her nuns and even over the famous prelates and theologians sitting in judgement on her state of prayer and her writings. Unless we accept the reality of this mysterious phenomenon operating in Teresa, we cannot understand her writings.

Although meant for our blessing, 'light on' has not proved an unmixed one, and this because it has not been recognised as *abnormal* and *not* the mystical grace itself. Because it fulfils a prophetic role in the church, it is the bearers of it who, by and large, are the masters of the spiritual life. They are the ones who have written about the path to God. This is not to say that all who have written on the mystical life are 'light on'. By no means: Teresa certainly was. It is possible but not certain that John of the Cross was also. It is true that we don't need this propheticism absolutely, all we need is to follow Jesus in the gospels and keep his commandments of love. However he chooses to give us light through one another, for our blindness and sinfulness hamper us continually. The 'light on', with their overwhelming sense of the reality of God helps us all. Those whose vocation is to a prolonged exposure to God in prayer, to a great inwardness, have a special need of the help of this charism. They can learn from these 'seers' what cannot otherwise be known. Enquiring man is always going to ask: 'What is union with God?' 'What is the mystical state?' 'What does it mean to say that Jesus and his Father come to *dwell* in the believers?' *How* is it? *What* goes on? Very, very few people know of these things by lived experience; these seers tell us as best they can. By and large, we intellectualise merely, we do not *know*. Only if we recognise this special gift operating in Teresa and acknowledge that it is not the mystical itself but only illuminating it, and, at the same time recognise the abundant upsurge of psychic energy triggered off by the 'sight' of the mystical happening, can we receive her precious wisdom, make use of that which her 'light on' was given for. As said, we won't find the clarification in Teresa herself, we have to sift for it. She was continually confusing three things: the mystical grace, her 'light on' experience of it, the psychic response, and not infrequently this confusion leads to absurdity. Let me illustrate: she is expatiating on the immense blessings infused contemplation brings with it and how could it be otherwise since it is as embrace of God himself, it is a 'spark of divine love enkindled in the soul', it's the 'purest gold of divine wisdom'. Very rightly we ask 'but would God offer this precious gift, which, after all, is only what Jesus is talking about as the gift of his Father he embodies, to the few only? We know it is offered to everyone who will accept it.

> You will desire, then, my daughters, to strive to attain this way of prayer and you will be right to do so, for, as I have said, the soul cannot fully understand the favours the Lord grants it there or the love which draws it ever nearer to himself.

She knows of only one way to obtain this favour (and this we can accept unreservedly as it is what our Lord himself teaches us), to practise what has been said in the earlier mansions and then try to be utterly humble. It is humility that obtains this grace. So far, so good. If we have this humility 'you will not think you merit these favours and consolations of the Lord or are likely to get them for as long as you live.' No distinction is present in her mind at this moment between the embrace of love, the nearness of God, the pure gold of divine wisdom and 'favours and

50

consolations'.

But how', you will ask, 'are we to gain them if we do not strive after them?' . . . There are several reasons why they should be striven for. The first is because the most essential thing is that we should love God without any motive of self-interest. The second is that there is some lack of humility in our thinking that in return for our miserable service we can obtain *anything so great* [italics mine, to draw attention to the clear reference to the 'gold of divine wisdom']. The third is because the true preparation for receiving these gifts is a desire to suffer and to imitate the Lord, not to receive *consolations* [italics mine]; for, after all, we have often offended him. The fourth reason is because His Majesty is not obliged to grant them to us, as he is obliged to grant us glory if we keep his commandments, without doing which we could not be saved, and he knows better than we do what is good for us and which of us truly love him. That is certain truth, as I know; and I also know people who walk the road of love, solely as they should, in order to serve Christ crucified, and not only do they neither ask for consolations nor desire them, but they beg him not to give them to them in this life. The fifth reason is that we should be labouring in vain; for this water does not flow through conduits as the other does . . . however much we may practise meditation, however much we may do violence to ourselves, and however many tears we shed, we cannot produce this water in those ways; it is given only to whom God wills to give it and often when the soul is not thinking about it at all.

The first three points and the fifth Teresa makes here are fault-less when they apply to the mystical grace itself. The fourth reveals the confusion. God is not obliged to grant 'them' to us as He is obliged to grant us glory if we keep his commandments. What does she mean by 'them'? In this instance the word must apply to 'favours and consolations' for, as we have already shown, the grace of infused contemplation is essential to holi-ness. This life giving 'touch' is the salvation which Jesus offers to all whereby we become children of God in very truth. Teresa concludes her reasons for not striving after – what? with, 'I am sure that if any of us achieve true humility and detachment . . . the Lord will not fail to grant us this favour (which one?) and many others which we shall not even know how to desire'. How utterly true this is of the gift of infused contemplation itself! At another time Teresa warns us that these 'favours' can be counterfeit. Anyone receiving them must make sure they are growing in humility, detachment, love of neighbour and all the virtues. If not, then they must be fearful and believe they are not of God, who when he visits the soul, always enriches it. Is it conceivable that the embrace of God, his life-giving touch, can be counterfeited? Who is like God? The divine touch must be of such a nature and at so profound a depth that imitation is impossible. What Teresa means here is that all sorts of 'experiences' may be had which are apparently identical with the effect of God's touch in her but which, in others, do not flow from this contact with God in the centre of the soul. She seems to suggest also that a genuine 'favour' which, again, she wrongly identifies with the divine touch, may, at times, foster pride, and warns us to be careful and to remember that everything is his gift. But surely this is quite absurd. How could the touch of Life itself harm us? It is as if we were saying that the healing touch of Jesus might serve to increase the leprosy! But as we have observed earlier and it is worth repeating, only too easily, 'favours' do induce a secret pride because it is assumed they are 'direct-God'. In themselves these things are of no great significance, and are of common occurence in many contexts, and can be stimulated in many ways, conscious and unconscious. Their presence *never* proves the divine touch; it is when we think they do that all sorts of illusions and dangers follow. Teresa constantly throws onto the scales of her ambiguity, the weight of the effects on a person's life. These in the last analysis – and of this she is absolutely sure – prove or disprove the reality of infused contemplation.

To strengthen the position we are maintaining in regard to 'experiences' which is of such great importance to a clear understanding of mysticism, it will be good to add the witness of one who was close to Teresa in her life time, who had reason to know her spiritual life, had read her writings and witnessed gross misunderstandings growing up around them – John of the Cross. I am not alone in detecting in John's work a deliberate if delicate corrective to mistaken interpretations of Teresa. Although he himself, as the *Spiritual Canticle* and *Living Flame* bear witness, knew the fire and the dance (though I think there is more to be said in reference to these two books but this is not the place for it), in his systematic exposition of the mystical life in the *Ascent* and *Dark Night*, he hammers home time and time again that infused contemplation of its very nature is hidden, most secret to the one receiving it. He counsels ruthless detachment from 'impressions, images, representations in which spiritual communications are involved' (or might be involved). This detachment 'from all that relates to its (the soul's) natural condition, the sensual and rational parts as well as the sensual', opens the soul to God's pure action, 'the deeper spirituality within'. He is certainly not detaching us from the deep communications of God; his purpose is to free us for these.

Lastly, we will call another witness, young, but wonderfully wise, Thérèse of Lisieux. Here is a mistress of spirituality every bit as much as her mother, Teresa of Avila. She trod a path totally barren of 'favours'. She lived in a religious milieu that assumed beyond question that 'favours' were the authenticating sign of great spirituality. Undismayed, perfectly content, she went her way. It wasn't a case of making the best of it. Rather, she grasped that her very darkness was Jesus' presence; that her experience was wholly authentic, a union with Jesus in his lowly manhood, *and that this is what union with God must mean in our mortal life*. She felt no need as did her brilliant mother, of countless directors to assure her of the truth of her way. It was uncomplicated by the dangerous tangle of undergrowth and overgrowth which, almost to the end, fostered a vague uneasiness in Teresa. But did not Jesus say: 'In that day you will *know* . . . you will not need to ask . . .'

Before we take up Teresa's text again, there is one more misunderstanding which obscures the truth of infused contemplation. Teresa is quite clear that we don't have this gift to begin with. Prayer, she says 'begins to be supernatural'. She adds that usually people have had to spend a considerable time in the earlier rooms of the castle before coming to this one where there is a *beginning* of supernatural prayer. In other words she assumes the need of a generous preparation – we have to prepare the soil for the precious seed. Popularly it is taken for granted that those of us who are baptised Christians, who try to serve God following our Lord, are already in the kingdom, we belong to those blessed ones who 'receive him' and are therefore made his children born not of flesh, not of the will of man but of God. In other words, we have received our new birth, our whole being is now supernatural and so is our prayer. Too easily, promise, potentiality have been expressed in terms of facts, fulfilment. If we look carefully at the gospels have we any reason for thinking that we, unlike others, have received the kingdom? Are we shown anyone in the gospels who actually did? Are we better than they? The point is that Jesus was rejected, even by his own. When the hour of scandal came they lost faith. Our baptism, the privilege of our Christian calling is affirming that *this* mystical union is what life is for, this is what God is calling us to do, this is our vocation. It is not a 'hey presto', it is done.

What we call the history of salvation is enacted, or should be, in every human heart. There is the stage of preparation, of promise. God sets to work to educate his sinful people, to give them some sort of knowledge of what he is like so that they can imitate him. It would be impossible without this long preparation for man to recognise, still less accept God as he is in himself. He reveals himself in signs and figures; through the events of history he trains and forms his people until the time has come for his direct intervention. This people can actually produce Jesus. Jesus, the most obedient son, is a product of this long formation. To him God can communicate himself totally. That is one side; on the other, in this Man, God himself is incarnate in his world, offering himself to men in the form of a servant, not – and this is of supreme importance, it lies at the very heart of a right understanding of infused contemplation – as the Lord of Glory. The climax of history has come, the crisis. Will man accept or reject their God? We know the answer. So terrible is the force of sin, of resistance to God in the human heart, that it crucified Jesus. But Jesus passed the test. He accepted his Father in his bitter suffering and death. This death proved the source of life for those who 'saw' God in this humiliated, suffering being. Jesus, having surrendered completely to his Father was received into his inmost heart, wholly transformed in his fires. He who was one with us, in flesh and blood like ours, suffering all the limitations of material being, is now Spirit and, as such, the source of Spirit for all his brethren. Through this Spirit men are transformed into God but in the same measure that they enter into the death/surrender of Jesus.

We, chronologically, are in the third era, that of Spirit. Jesus has lived, was crucified and is now risen. We live in the new age. But we must be careful in our thinking. It is of relatively little moment that we live in the new age chronologically. What matters is that we do so in reality. Just as the vast numbers living in the era of Jesus historically speaking were not so in reality but still in the era of the old testament, so with us. Each of us begins in the old testament and maybe we never move out of it in this life; it will depend on our desire. We are invited to do so – the preparation is preparation *for* something, not a value in itself. To move out of it involves really accepting Jesus and this means 'earthquake', the overturning of our world, the end of it, a death in order to rise to the new life in Jesus, which means that then we will be *in reality* in the era of Spirit. We can see here the scriptural foundations for the traditional teaching that there are three ages or three stages in the Christian life. Those who have entered deeply into the mystery of God and man know that this is so, they know it cannot be otherwise through the very nature of things. In Teresa's terminology, the first three mansions are the old testament of the soul, the preparation for the visitation of God; it is religion of the 'flesh'. The fourth, fifth and sixth are the soul's encounter with the suffering Son of Man, a sharing in his death. The seventh is the risen life, the age of the Spirit, when all is Spirit.

Fourth Mansion, Part II

Teresa puts us on the alert with her opening sentences. What she has described so far is relatively simple but now the task facing her is complex for she must try to describe a work no longer human but divine. An entirely new element is coming into being and she warns us that we shall be in danger of misunderstanding her unless we ourselves have considerable experience of it. This new thing is intimately connected with the king who dwells in the heart of the castle. The rooms into which Teresa now brings us are really inside the castle – the others were merely outer courts – and therefore something of the radiance and beauty of the king reaches us. We cannot come to these more interior rooms, she says, until we have lived for a long time in the outer ones, learning, so to speak, the manners of the king's court. The preparation, the old testament of the individual, preparing to receive his God in person. Now is the hour and moment; now the Lord begins to give us his kingdom, simply because now we are in a position to recognise it and welcome it. The first grace of infused or mystical contemplation is given.

In order to understand Teresa and so benefit by her guidance, we must discern carefully the very heart of the grace she is describing from the unimportant accompaniments we have already discussed. We have to remember also that she is viewing it as 'light on' and this will make her actual experience of it totally different from ours. Nevertheless, it is precisely this 'light on' view that enables her to see what is happening and this is the greatest help to us. Let us then look first of all, at what she describes of her own experience. Typically she begins with telling us just what it felt like – very, very different from the feeling experience of former times. She goes to some length to clarify this. The feeling experiences of the earlier mansions she

56

calls 'spiritual sweetness', those of the fourth and later mansions, 'spiritual consolations'. Buried in her contrasting descriptions of both experiences is the essential core of difference between the two stages. In the former what is experienced flows through the ordinary channels of communication – like water flowing rather noisily through conduits into a basin. In the latter, the water flows *straight from the source*, not merely filling the basin but overflowing onto all around it. Recall for a moment what has been said of 'light on'. It reveals God in the soul, shows what he is doing. Thus Teresa, in this mysterious way, 'saw' God present, loving her, embracing her. She speaks of something happening in her depth. What had happened before – she sees clearly – was not in her 'interior depths' (they were not there), but was all to do with her thoughts and feelings about God, her good works, her grief over her sins; that is with natural activity concentrated on the things of God. Now, it isn't she who is doing the work at all, something *happens* in her depth. In her case, every particle of her being responded with spontaneous delight; psyche and body participated in the feast of love. She seems to make no distinction between this blissful felt experience and the actual grace. The water seems to be at one and the same time the grace itself and the delightful feeling. But note the inevitable ambiguity which forces her into difficult positions. At the very outset of this mansion she informs us that the reptiles from the moat cannot do the same harm here as in former mansions. Nevertheless they harass and upset us and force us to struggle. This is a boon, she says. It would be dangerous for us to be in this state of consolation always and she is suspicious of any prolonged absorption in it. Rightly we may object that, if this consolation is the mystical grace it cannot possibly harm us even though it were permanent, and is it possible for the devil to counterfeit a truly mystical grace?

Teresa then is sure that what is happening to her is, in fact, the king, in her inmost centre, making his presence felt. The automatic reaction is a state of great peace, and delight. (Prayer of quiet). But the important thing from the human side, from our side, is that the 'will' is united to God. Whatever we may feel and think, says Teresa, there is ultimately only one way of knowing that the will has known this union with God, and that is the effects of this prayer and the actions which follow. These will prove or disprove that we are more grounded in, dedicated to, God. What does Teresa mean by 'will'? After all, we cannot really speak of ourselves as having a will, having intellect and so forth. If my will is choosing God it means that this human consciousness which is me, is choosing God, and this human consciousness cannot choose unless it is knowing. Thus to speak as if the will could be occupied with God while the understanding is not is a contradiction. However, the point Teresa is making is important and we must try to grasp it. What we usually mean by will and understanding relates to our material being, commensurate with ourselves. As we have tried to explain, to begin with there is nothing more to us than this materiality. We are 'flesh' in the scriptural sense. When we relate to God consciously, when we pray we do so with what we are: we try to know him and love him within the bounds of what we are, which is 'flesh'. But what is happening in this mansion is transcending this materiality. A new dimension of being is evolving. Though Teresa speaks of progression within to what is already there, we say a new mansion is coming into existence and this has the quality of 'spirit'. A new sort of life is beginning with its own needs and its own operations and these latter are not circumscribed by material limitations. Again, it isn't that we have a deeper will, a more searching understanding than hitherto; rather, the evolving being that is me is being given a divine knowledge of God and inevitably leaps up to embrace Love showing himself in uniting himself to me. As the divine contact is utterly secret from 'flesh' – the latter *cannot* know of it so – so is the human response which now likewise partakes of spirit. Only 'light on' can actually 'see' this new dimension of being and its response to the divine encounter.

Teresa describes a grace which seems to absorb the whole of her. Then a sort of split state. She still sees that the 'will' is absorbed in God but 'thought' is not absorbed, it wanders here there and everywhere. She admits herself that it was not until she reached the seventh mansion that she really understood what was happening at this time. She distinguishes between understanding and thought. If 'will' is occupied, so must 'under-standing' be, for the first is impossible without the second. The evolving spiritual self is occupied with its Love, but thought – that is the material mind which formerly has had a good, worthy job – now finds itself redundant and, highly indignant makes all the fuss it can, interferes, wanders around dabbling in every-thing.

So much for a 'light on' experience. Now for ourselves. Two burning questions: what is the normal experience of the first mystical graces; and, can we know we have received them? The answer to the first is that experience will be precisely *non-experience* in the usual, popular sense of the term and the reason is very simple, based on the nature of the grace itself as we have already stressed. An encounter has taken place in the depth of being, in the growing point of spirit, and human con-sciousness, essentially material, can know nothing of it direct-ly. To say the experience is precisely non-experience is not the same thing as saying there is no experience. Non-experience *is* a sort of experience. But no amount of spiritual feeling, no matter how sublime, no matter how closely it seems to tally with what Teresa describes, is an experience of the grace itself. Does this mean then that we can never know it save through the rare phenomenon of 'light on'? Do those advanced in the spiri-tual way not know it at all? The answer is that they do know it but do not know how they know or what they know. What is more, we have to say, I think, that they do not know it at the time it happens but only, looking back, they know it has hap-pened. Sometime in their life they are going to know. This is certain. However, at this moment we are considering very early graces and of these we must say I think that they cannot be known. But they are not without effects and these can be known though perhaps we ourselves cannot evaluate them cor-rectly.

God wills us to keep our eyes closed and not seek to peer into his face. Any attempt of that kind would lead to illusions which are only a form of idol making. Think of his word to Moses, 'you cannot see my face; for man shall not see me and live ... Behold, there is a place by me where you shall stand upon the rock; and while my glory passes by I will put you in a cleft in the rock and I will cover you with my hand until I have passed by; then I will take away my hand, and you shall see my back; but my face shall not be seen'. A true picture of what must be. During the encounter we are sheltered by the darkness of his outstretched hand; we see nothing; when he has passed by, then we know of his passing, not at first, perhaps, but as we correspond and grow and these encounters increase in number and depth; we being to 'know' the Lord, his inmost nature. He has given us a face to look at and that is the face of his human Son, but this face, also, we can only really know from within, from this deep encounter. We might say that this Son is the cleft in the rock where we are put in order to meet God in his unmediated being. The unbearable presence is made bearable in Jesus.

In the mystical encounter, however fleeting, the deep self has had a glimpse of Reality itself and cannot but spurn imitation. The moment passes but in some way the self can never forget this glimpse and its experience is coloured by it. One of the effects is what we normally call aridity. The growing spiritual being within is now impatient of the coarse food the mind supplies. Hence a sense of aridity, distaste. Spurned by the inner self, useless, empty, the ordinary channels of communication echo hollowly with every kind of noise and disturbance whilst the choosing self feeds secretly on divine food.

We cannot conclude from this however, that aridity, distractions and inner misery are necessarily the result of mystical prayer. Other criteria have to be applied as we have remarked so often. Teresa knows that this interior turmoil will vary with our states of health and with our temperament and so forth. Not everyone will suffer from it so keenly as she did. Her passionate, highly charged psychic makeup must have been extremely vulnerable, and most likely the 'light on' mystical graces together with their psychic counterparts, may well have increased this vulnerability. How she must have longed, at least unconsciously, for rapture, when, as she would say, the Lord himself stilled the tumultuous inner sea, holding her mind and senses absorbed in him. For her, conditioned as she was to expect that a vivid feeling of God's presence, was the authentication of a truly mystical life, this turmoil and aridity must have been daunting, creating a sense of insecurity which seems always ready to surface! No wonder she found it hard to come to terms with the problem. It took her a long time, as she tells us; no one managed to reassure her completely. Eventually she saw the answer for herself but it was only when she was in the seventh mansion. She is anxious that we should learn from her experience and avoid unnecessary anxiety. We must not worry, she insists, about the wanderings of our minds. 'The soul may perhaps be wholly united with Him in the mansions very near His presence, while thought remains in the outskirts of the castle, suffering a thousand wild and venomous creatures and from this suffering winning merit.' Thought, in the sense Teresa means, *can* only be in the outer courts. It belongs there. Teresa declares this painful turmoil one of the hardest things to bear, greater than scorn and other outward trials. Misery within makes outward trials weigh much more heavily.

To support the effects of mystical prayer, both in 'light on' and 'light off' is going to call for great generosity. We are concerned now only with 'light off'. If we undertake prayer in order to get something out of it for ourselves, save only a growth in love of God, then we can never receive him. This is why over this stage hangs the cross of Christ symbolising man's affirmation that God is all and man is nothing save insofar as he is a for-Godness: our innate desire to seek a fulfilment within ourselves, within the created world, must be totally surrendered; we must die to our material way of being, bounded by our senses, our natural judgments, our deciding for ourselves what is our happiness and seeking it. We have to consent with all our heart to be drawn beyond ourselves into a sphere of God which, though it is ultimately our total beatitude and sole fulfilment, is alien, frightening and painful to our limited corporality. What we read of in scripture of the birth pangs of the age to come, what we see of Jesus' own dying, is telling us of what it means for human beings to surrender to the divine invasion of love. Our basically sinful 'flesh' cries out that 'it is a fearful thing to fall into the hands of the living God', and it remains a sad fact that most of us resist to the end of our days the God who would draw us into the depths of his own life. We have to learn to love God more than ourselves, resigning ourselves into his hands, accepting in blind faith that what he ordains, all that he does, is for our ultimate happiness and fulfilment. We have to sacrifice the desire to know if we have received mystical grace and the security we think that would give us; sacrifice too the longing to know where we are on the journey. We have to banish from our hearts everything but the naked desire for God alone. In the measure that we do this we are utterly safe. Without delay, with absolute certainty, God will accomplish his will in us. But we find this so hard to believe when nothing seems to happen. We can't really trust God.

What will an hour of prayer be like when our mind can give us nothing to use to 'put myself in the presence of God', to contemplate him? Naturally, by sheer instinct, by all we are, we reach out to God in thought and the follow-up of desire. There is no other way for us but that. Let us say we have been in earnest, have really tried in every way we can think of to do what God asks and that we go to prayer with as pure a motive as possible – to want God and him alone. But when we go to prayer there is nothing there. Of course we can think thoughts, we could take a book and help ourselves to find good thoughts to move our will to want God, but these thoughts are empty, dead as dodos. How then do we 'get in touch with God'? How are we to think of him? Where is he? Is he anywhere? Here we are, a solid block of flesh, kneeling or sitting in church or somewhere else. Everything is solid and real around us – the walls, the sound of life outside, voices, cars. That is our world, in a short time we will be back in it again. What is real? How unreal, insubstantial, seems the notion of God and prayer to him. Nothing, nothing whatever to assure us of his presence, of the value of what we are doing. This is when so many give up or, if they don't give up completely, retreat from where they are, determining to make prayer more alive, more interesting, more obviously the 'real thing'. They may succeed in convincing themselves that now, at last, they have something – this is the real thing! They are mistaken. The only way forward is into mystery which is extremely painful. We crave for what is suited to us, what we can understand, can encompass, for what gives us a sense of security and worthwhileness. The mystery which is God gives us none of these things on the level at which we want them. We are being summoned to the espousals of the cross.

At this disconcerting time we have to recall what prayer is all about, what is its essence. It is God being God for us, self-squandering love, offering himself at every moment. On our side it is nothing but a resolve to be there to receive that love. If only we could keep firm hold of this truth, there would be no problem. We would always know what to do and would need no one's advice. What we actually do at prayer would be the right thing even though we lack the assurance that it is so from a human point of view. We shall deal with every obstacle in such a way that it becomes a positive help. But alas, we are not single-minded nor is our faith strong and thus we create a thousand complexities for ourselves of which the object is not the love of God but how to satisfy ourselves.

We have to exercise our faith. There is no other answer. This is what God asks. 'Don't measure me by your own miserable standards', he says. 'Let me be God in my own way. Can't you trust me?' The words of Jesus which, if we choose, reveal to us the face of God, must be our constant food. It is these which must nourish our faith. 'But we do all this', we say, 'and we are dead. Nothing happens'. What do we expect to happen? What could happen that could give us the security we crave? Nothing, because anything that happened cognisible to sense, would not be God and would carry within it no assurance. There is no answer save that our God is the God he is. We may feel dead, but must ignore our feelings, make up our minds to live on the revelation of Jesus not on our own subjective reactions. When we think about it, what a horrifying thing it is to do, to stand in our own subjective world! There is only one real world and that is the world Jesus reveals to us, a world of utter love and security which he has made our own.

If we make up our minds to it and come faithfully day after day to our tryst of prayer, we are acting out superb faith. Is there any greater affirmation that God is all, that he is our sole meaning, than these hours of prayer? Not hours bathed in delight, not hours of stirring, interesting thoughts and emotions, not hours of pleasant, soothing absorption, but hours of human tedium where we seem to get no returns. As far as this world and its values goes, this is dead loss, wasted time. In our fidelity to it we are saying in effect, 'you are my God and my all. Unless you possess me wholly I am meaningless'. This prayer is a cry of our very being, an invitation to God to be in very truth our God. Will he ignore this cry of being, so costly to 'flesh'? 'Will not God vindicate his elect, who cry to him day and night? Will he delay long over them? I tell you, he will vindicate them speedily . . .' but note the sad afterthought, 'nevertheless, when the Son of Man comes, will he find faith on earth?'

An increase of faith is part of the 'dilation' of heart which, Teresa says, is the direct effect of the divine encounter. We must be able to discern it. It is this growth in faith which lies behind the idea of 'being held'. Faith is not so much a grasp of truths of faith and assent to them, though this is part of it; faith is a 'knowing' not 'about God' but a knowing God – an obscure, secret knowledge which is the source of one's living. It is not something felt, it is not a clarity of mind or a sense of firmness of will in assent; it is a 'being held' which makes us hold on in darkness and bewilderment, when commonsense, all that we ordinarily mean by experience, draws a blank. Faith holds us within, in our inmost citadel, without rhyme or reason, it seems. Here, for the discerning, is proof of the presence of at least the beginning of the mystical. Below the level of sense and reason, a life is going on, secret from the person himself, revealing itself in wisdom, not verbal but in the science of life. There is a 'quality' of life, unmistakable to those with experience, far removed from showiness, the desire to impress others or to be among the advanced. Its essential accompaniment will be real humility.

There will be growth in generosity. In Teresa's day, 'penances', by which were meant corporal acts of penance much in vogue, were considered the hallmarks of generosity. You did what you ought, fulfilled your obligations, then if you were generous, you went beyond them, and the accepted form of this 'over and above' was a range of corporal penances. We cannot share this esteem for self-inflicted corporal penance but the principle remains. The mystical grace shows itself in increasing generosity, a real gift of self, a growing resolution to put self aside and devote oneself utterly to others; a gift of self that will persevere in prayer in spite of boredom, the sense of uselessness and growing sense of sinfulness. It may well be a 'poor' generosity, a trembling, frightened one, but all the more truly generous for the natural shrinking. There are lots of seemingly generous acts that are not necessarily so, they can be full of self-seeking. What we are meaning is a resolution to pay the price, to give God everything he asks whatever the cost. This is the passion of love growing in the heart, a 'spark of divine love'. As Teresa points out, profound faith, humility, generosity, are not normally the fruit of a single mystical encounter. This 'dilation' is the result of many such encounters faithfully responded to.

We are still very, very weak, certainly not strong enough to take risks and we must ensure that we protect with every care, the precious graces we are entrusted with. A common temptation will be to escape the growing sense of ineffectualness. We will find ourselves saying we want to give God more than this – much more prayer, greater solitude or greater activity. Let us be infinitely careful less, far from giving God more, we are giving him less, insisting in giving what he is not asking. We can want the satisfaction that comes from feeling we can teach and guide others in the spiritual path. It can afford us an authentication, we think. We can wear ourselves down in the apostolate to the neglect of prayer because this arid distracted sort of prayer seems unsatisfactory; it leaves us feeling poor specimens, spiritually speaking. If we neglect prayer we are like the unweaned child taken from its mother's breast and given no substitute. Teresa becomes singularly grave in her warning and lament. She has seen it happen, people brought so far, given this special gift of God and then failing in one way or another. Most often they will not give up in the obvious sense, still pursuing what we call a spiritual life, but they fail by deviation, swerving from the straight path of pure love and trust into subtle self-seeking. She warns us that our temptations will be more subtle and powerful and our responsibility far greater than those of others, for we have been given more, for others as well as for ourselves. We have much to answer for.

A casual reading of St Teresa could give the impression of irrelevance. 'All this talk about mystical prayer and states of prayer! As irrelevant as moving deck chairs around while the ship is sinking!'. Well, if we are paying attention to states of feeling and 'favours', then the criticism is justified, but if we grasp what Teresa is really talking about in infused contemplation, then we see it is the very life-line, our very meaning as human beings. It is God himself bringing man to himself, sharing his own way of being with him. It is more a question of letting down the lifeboats to save all on board.

There is no doubt that 'favours' were highly esteemed by Teresa and she greatly enjoyed them, but what we must insist on is that this was so only because in her case the ground of them was a profound communication of God. She was unable to distinguish. She knew God was giving himself, knew with complete certainty, for she 'saw' him, and her whole being thrilled with the contact. Of the first she could not speak, even to herself; of the latter, all that happened in her psyche and body, she could; this was something she could look at and analyse. Then the confusion begins and multiplies. Others tell her of what happens to them. She looks at their life and because it does not show the fruits she expects of such intimate contact with God, she is bound to declare their 'favours' counterfeit. But, as human experiences they are as genuine as hers; the difference is that while hers were induced by the radiation of the inner grace, these others were not. She outlines for us one such pseudo experience, an absorption which could be confused with such as she knew in the prayer of quiet. It lasts far too long to be genuine, in her opinion. There are no fruits, no ensuing wisdom. What she seems unable to conclude is that the phenomenon is basically the same as hers, the same metal, but cast by a different mint.

In spite of her preoccupation with 'favours', Teresa never loses her singlemindedness. By a miracle of grace she swam unscathed (or almost) through these dangerous shoals. She wanted God; what happened to her, increased her love for God whether it was 'favours' or trials. 'Favours' seemed to inspire her with greater courage and generosity and bred humility. How could she not desire them? But we note that she never sought for these delightful feelings. She never consciously tried to foster them – she was convinced this is impossible, try as we may. She is wrong here; what she means is that no matter what we do we can never acquire infused contemplation, this is very true, but it is possible to attain all sorts of psychic awareness if one sets one's mind to it. For some perhaps it is more difficult than for others because of temperament. Even the unconscious esteem and desire for 'experiences' induce them. Teresa, it seems, was often deceived by what others told her of their prayer. 'Light on' revealed her own soul and what God was doing there. When she tried to use this knowledge universally, she made big mistakes. Her tendency is to credulity, to think others more advanced than they are because they talk well and use the same vocabulary as herself and boast the same states of feeling. More blantant impostures she could see but not the unconscious self-delusion of really good people. Her tendency is always to over-estimate good people.

Teresa's singlemindedness is markedly revealed in her deprecation of any studied approach to prayer, any contriving, any painful efforts to produce a state, techniques of one kind or another. These offend her sense of truth. They are self-centred, all the attention is on the self. We want something, want to experience something. This has nothing to do with real prayer which is a surrender of self and self-interest. We are mis-understanding entirely the essence of prayer which is an opening of ourselves for God to give himself to us. We are trying to lay hold of God, to grab him, but it isn't God we are after only a feeling, an experience that 'exalts'. This contriving reveals that we think God can be had only by extraordinary means, that he is not the ever-giving God. After all, to pursue these techniques usually calls for high intelligence and leisure; that is, they are only for an élite. What is more, how often we could be neglecting self-evident duties in order to have the leisure for these practices. Take a contemplative religious, for instance. Their day is carefully scheduled: Office, periods of private prayer, work for the support of the community and others. The only time possible would be that devoted to private prayer. How very, very easily this period, intended to be exclusively God's, just so that he can have us there poor and surrendered, would be taken up with self, with things, not with God; with techniques, states of feeling of one kind or another. There is great danger of using this sacred time for self-culture. All this must be interpreted correctly. Some of the techniques can be used to help us to be quiet before God, but we have to understand that they are only natural techniques and keep them in their place. Once again, singlemindedness can be our only guide and safety. 'We must love God without any motive of self-interest'. We must be ready to suffer and imitate our Lord, not to crave for consolations. 'I cannot believe in the efficacy of human activity in matters where His Majesty appears to have set limits to it and to have been pleased to reserve action to himself'. What she has particularly in mind is the effort to silence thought, even going to the length of holding one's breath in the attempt as though the cessation of thought is a necessity for passive prayer.

Throughout her writings Teresa gives practical help for our conduct in prayer and particularly how to deal with our minds. As already said, in the early stage of prayer, before any mystical grace has intervened, the mind has an all-important role. At the bidding of the heart it must labour to furnish motives and strong convictions for loving and serving God. Because it is God's deep desire to give himself, since he is this very desire, and we exist solely to be the happy recipients of his love, it goes without saying that he will give himself whenever and wherever and in the measure that it is possible. Thus when we are really in earnest, steadily pursuing God's will, it will not be long before we are given his life-giving touch. We will be unaware of the fact and we do not need to know of it. We leave God to do his part and concentrate on ours. It is a misconception to think that we need to know when the mystical life begins because then we have to change our way of praying and this, largely, means we must cease to meditate. If we have grasped the nature of prayer, that it is God giving himself and we receiving him, we won't fall into this error. We will use the mind humbly, gently, reflectively, always doing that which 'most arouses us to love. But perhaps we do not know what love is; it would not surprise me a great deal to learn this, for love consists not in the extent of our happiness but in the firmness of our determination to please God in everything'. If we are looking for an immediate, discernible end for prayer, there it is: we aim at fostering determination to give ourselves to God. We must never deliberately give up meditation whilst it is helping us to this. It is simply not true to say that in the advanced stages of prayer we cease to use our minds. How self-conscious we would be if we had to follow rules, and how it would destroy all sense of relationship. Prayer must mean forgetfulness of self, not a watching of self in order to detect how we are praying, what is happening to us, how we feel, etc. We do what best urges us to love God and our neighbour.

Without in anyway undercutting what has just been said, it remains a fact that one of the effects of mystical prayer is to lessen the importance of the mind at prayer. What is likely to happen is that, at least from time to time, we simply cannot think useful thoughts, nothing helps us and we are in a state of rootless helplessness which is hard to bear because drab and unsatisfying. Yet the mind will still go on working because that is its function; it seizes on any subject matter available. It isn't that we choose to give up meditation, it forsakes us. When we feel this impotence, it is useless trying to flog our mind into action. We must endeavour to stay in prayer, offering ourselves to God, accepting the painful awareness of indigence. On the one hand we must not strain after effects, on the other, we must not fall into inertia. What we must do is to keep in mind as best we can that we are with God and that he is the God who loves us. We can count utterly on him. In other words, exercise our faith. This is to make use of the understanding as Teresa means it. She advised us not to be disturbed by wandering thoughts, our heart has to keep throwing itself into the arms of love unseen, unfelt, but most surely love. It is foolish to waste our energy trying to control the mind and fretting over its vagaries. We must accept the sense of unworthiness that our disordered mind brings upon us.

Whilst we must not go avidly seeking satisfying thoughts but must remain quiet, exposed, surrendered, nevertheless, in one way or another our minds must work all our life long: helpful or tormenting, it is part of our human condition and must be accepted wholeheartedly. Even were it to happen that we find ourselves in a state of emotional happiness or psychic aware-ness – it may be emanating from a divine contact, but it need not be so – Teresa counsels us still to use our minds a little and not to allow ourselves to fall into a state of inertia and stupidity. We can be so delighted with our feelings, so taken up with them, that we are not taking notice of God. The fundamental act of prayer on the human side is the act of surrender, and this always involves an act of the mind averting to his presence.

The term 'passive prayer' is often misunderstood. It is taken to mean that we enter a state of emotional and mental passivity; that the passivity in question is on the conscious level. This is a misconception. Passive prayer is infused prayer and as we have persistently pointed out, it is infused at a level below our con-scious mind. Its reception is absolutely secret from the mind and senses and we must not forget that, at this stage, it is a fleet-ing grace. Its reception does not require one form of prayer rather than another. It is not something we do, it is what God does in us. He touches us, we do not have to strain out to take hold of him – such a reluctant lover! He puts the food into our mouths without our knowing it, into that spiritual being which is only now emerging and of which our mind and senses can have no direct knowledge. This is life hidden with Christ in God. Many called upon to discern in spiritual matters use the term 'being held' as a criterion for discerning the presence of infused prayer. By this they usually mean some sort of mental or psychic absorption, something experienced on the con-scious level. There is some truth in the notion that 'being held' is a criterion for mystical prayer as already suggested in regard to faith, but this being held is not on the felt level. It is a question of the soul 'becoming'. Under the touch of God it is quickened into being. This beginnings of a new self has its own life and its own needs. Something is happening in the evolving soul that manifests itself in the quality of its Christian committment, but its germinal point cannot be caught hold of and looked at. The way of being of the becoming self is that of Jesus; his vision, his values, his fortitude and constancy, and these often seem alien to the conscious self. Self is being taken over by, held by, this mysterious life within, increasing in the measure that the loving, transforming action of God meets with a generous response. This is far removed from states of feeling, absorbtion in prayer, 'becoming a contemplative', having 'a facility for prayer' and so forth.

'I have written at great length of this mansion as it is the one which the greatest number of souls enter'. If we understand the fourth mansion as the first encounters with 'pure God', then it does seem right to affirm that most people who live in a serious, responsible, generous life, enter it – enter it, but not necessarily learn to live in it. We have tried to examine the reason for this failure in the chapter 'The Hold-up' in *Guidelines for Mystical Prayer*. Few respond generously to the first divine encounters and thus never grow so as to receive more. They choose to stay at an earlier stage. In the moment of encounter, the will is united to God. The growing point of spirit, leaps irresistibly up at the call of Life; the choosing self cannot but enfold its Love. What should follow is a greater determination and generosity to live in accordance with this new dynamism, and this is what does not happen in many cases. The becoming 'new self' abdicates shamefully to the 'old self', the dear familiar old. If we would go on then we must learn to disregard the complaints, and clamours, the fears and cowardice of the 'old self'.

Teresa knows that self-interest in prayer is one of the main obstacles to growth. We undertake a life of prayer more for what we can get out of it – though we may not face up to the fact – than to hand ourselves over to God. Hence we simply cannot accept the situation when this self-interest is not served. Teresa never saw with the clarity of John of the Cross the impediment of 'spiritual riches'. He took his sword and slashed away at everything that was not pure love. It is more than likely that much of his zeal was aroused by the self-indulgence of his fellow-religious, men and women, influenced by an erroneous interpretation of their great mother's writings. However, in her own way, if we want to see it, Teresa has quite a lot to say on the subject. It is worth remarking that for her the fourth mansion is a suffering one. True, she gives us a description of psychic delight but there are pages on trouble and suffering. One of her chief concerns is to reassure and encourage us on what is a hard path. When she introduces us to this stage she points out that it is certainly not free from difficulties and temptations. Reptiles from the moat still get in and harass us, but now they serve as occasions for learning humility and exerting ourselves for love's sake. It is a mistaken notion to think that the spiritual goal we are moving towards is one of felt peace lifted up above the storms of earth, sustained by an abiding sense of God's presence, an Eden restored. We are far better off when we are forced to come to grips with our secret vices, perverted motivations and general sinfulness. To come closer to the king means always a clearer revelation of our sinfulness and a summons to do something about it, to change. We have to struggle with all we are to root out the evil that is in us even though we know, and continually experience, that we can never succeed of ourselves.

With her love for classification, Teresa describes a form of prayer which seems closely allied to what she calls the prayer of quiet but it is not, she thinks, identified with it. She calls it the prayer of recollection. It is clear to see, that Teresa distinguishes it from the former for no other reason than that the bodily response of each differs. In the first it is very intense, in this, the prayer of recollection, it is not. At the heart of both, in her case, lies a genuine mystical grace of identical nature. What she says of this prayer of recollection is worth examination. If we abstract from the unimportant bodily reaction, we see that it is a gathering up of the powers within the self in order to surrender the whole self to God. We are scattered beings, disintegrated, torn with conflicting desires, drawn hither and thither. God's loving encounter has the effect of drawing us together, making us whole. Love is born of it and this love begins to dominate our wandering desires, calling them within to the one sole Good, ordering everything to the service of love. Gradually it masters them all and so one is recollected, gathered up, living always from one's centre, always directed to God and choosing him. This is the end of dissipation and wasted time and energy.

It was on the feast of the Presentation of our Lord that I began to examine the fourth mansion and the thought of Simeon was much in mind. Teresa herself recalls him when she is writing of the prayer of quiet in the *Way of Perfection*. Simeon stands for the welcome God has a right to expect of us when he comes to us. Simeon lived in expectation. His life had meaning only as expectation of his Lord's coming. This is the meaning of human life on earth but for how many of us is it really so? His singlemindedness makes him sensitive to the promptings of the Spirit and under this impulsion he comes into the temple. 'The just man, Simeon, saw no more than the glorious Infant – a poor little child, Who to judge from the swaddling clothes in which he was wrapped and from the small number of the people he had as a retinue to take him up to the temple, might well have been the son of these poor people rather than the Son of the Heavenly Father.' It was God Simeon wanted, not himself and therefore he did not dictate the terms on which he would welcome him; he was ready to accept his Lord however he chose to come. Thus he was able to recognise Jesus for what he was. He was perfectly satisfied, his life was fulfilled, the kingdom was his. Oh, the scandal of ordinariness! How few there are who are not thrown by it at least at sometime or other! Yet the gospel carries this lesson: the Son of Man has risen from the dead, everything is changed at depth but the world goes on as if nothing had happened. This is what faith is all about. In this moment of immense significance, when the Lord breaks into our world in power we feel the same, look the same. Why do we assume that it should not be like that? We want to substitute a golden calf for the God of mystery. This mystery of God is always met in Jesus and nowhere else. A little earlier we have spoken of 'pure God'. We can only have 'pure God' in Jesus. Only through Jesus does 'pure God' touch us and we touch him.

Fifth Mansion

Can anyone read through the four chapters of the fifth mansions without a sense of ambiguity if of confusion? It is due to the limitation we have pointed out earlier, Teresa's inability to discern the distinction between the actual mystical grace itself, what she 'saw' of it through her endowment of 'light on', and her psychic response to both. To her, it seems, all three were one experience, the 'prayer of union'. Her attention is in great part absorbed by the psychic accompaniment and this is not to be wondered at as it is the only thing she could talk about even to herself. It is the most interesting part, at any rate! At first glance we might deduce that what distinguishes the fifth mansion from the fourth is the intensity of this psychic reaction. Her preoccupation with this element of her experience, the least important, in fact, allows her to think that many enter these fifth mansions, that very few do not; some go further in than others, some only reach the door.

Predisposed as she was to believe that these psychic states are part and parcel of the mystical grace and necessarily accompany growing intimacy with God, receiving the confidences of others regarding their own, similar experiences, she was only too ready to accept that the identical psychic state argued to the same depth of grace. Possibly most of these communications were by letter or by a passing exchange. She was not in a position to apply her ultimate criterion as to the reality of the virtues of the one in question. The people of her acquaintance were as predisposed as she was to expect 'experiences', probably many of them were 'sensitives' and reacted in this way to spiritual things. It is likely that in some cases the 'experience' was an effect of some mystical grace but no one could know that for certain. Because she readily accepted that experiences like her own arose from the same grace, she was bewildered by the fact that they did not bear the expected fruit. This failure preoccupies her throughout this mansion. Of course she is ready to admit that people can be deceived by the devil who disguises himself as an angel of light but clearly she is at a loss to explain the matter fully.

It would seem certain in Teresa's case that the intensity of her psychic response did correspond with the power and depth of the new grace. It is the nature of this newness that we must examine. She expatiates on the wonders to be described, the 'treasures and delights' to be found in this mansion. But can she say anything worthwhile about them, she wonders; is it not better to keep silent? No, she must try to say something, however inadequate, as others are looking to her for guidance.

We must note exactly what Teresa has to tell us of the 'light on' insight – what she sees is happening in the 'prayer of union'. We shall see that there is a difference between this and what happened in the fourth mansion. There 'His Majesty' had 'drawn near, was 'close,' the soul was 'in his presence,' 'very close to him'. Here 'His Majesty is in such close contact and union with the essence of the soul. . . . God implants Himself in the interior of the soul . . .' 'His Majesty must put us right into the centre of our soul, and must enter there Himself . . .'

At this point I think it very important to stress again that the state of 'light on' is *extremely* rare and that all of us would be wise to take for granted that we belong to 'light off'. I seem to be harping on the same string but experience has brought home to me how easily these things are misunderstood. Not a few people of my own acquaintance are certain they have undergone an experience such as Teresa describes fulsomely in this mansion. That may be true, no one could say 'nay', such things are not uncommon and can take place totally outside a religious context. However, what they are talking about is a psychic reaction, it is not 'light on'. What is more, it is also clear that the psychic experience in their case, did not flow from the 'prayer of union' because we do not see the fruits of this 'prayer of union'. We are dealing with the deepest realities of human existence and to be trivial, self-seeking, indulging in play-

75

acting even if unconscious, is abhorrent. We must stand in the truth even at great cost. If we do not, there is no chance whatever of progress which means being drawn into the blinding Truth.

In the few phrases enshrining Teresa's effort to give some form to the ineffable insight, we get the idea of a new 'region' where the encounter with God is taking place. It isn't just 'soul' in the commonly accepted notion of the term, of this she is certain; a new depth, a new region, unknown before, is revealed. It is here that a bewildering intimacy is enacted. God has not entered by any conceivable channel of communication or knowledge, through the senses, through the mind. No, the doors and windows are tight shut and he is there, in the room! The 'sight' of this intimacy throws Teresa into rapture and, we observe, she acted out in her body and psyche, a sort of dramatisation of it. Because of our conviction that this bodily representation is totally unimportant, no time will be spent dwelling on it. We are interested only in the grace itself. The moment of this unspeakable encounter is of brief duration, being a 'visit' of the Lord, not a permanent abiding, but the effects are profound and lasting.

Teresa speaks of 'certainty which remains in the soul, which can be put there only by God ... how, you will ask, can we become so convinced of what we have not seen?' That I do not know; it is the work of God.' This certainty, which we realise is of a very special quality (beware, 'sensitives', note the word 'special'), is precisely the effect of 'light on' and can be had in no other way. Of course we can all be certain of God, of spiritual truths, by faith. We can be certain too that we have had a startling psychic experience of what we might call 'God's presence'. This is not what is in question. The certainty Teresa has in mind in this instance is of a different kind altogether. Were we not obliged to speak of 'light on' and its special function and features, it would be wise to leave it untouched. However, we are obliged because in Teresa, whom we are expounding, we have a 'light on' person who gives us her 'light on' experience. Significantly, the object of her certainty in this instance is that 'God has been in the soul and the soul has been in God'. This, oddly, did not square with what she had learned in doctrinal instruction. Hitherto, she had not grasped that God is present in all things by 'presence, power and essence'; she had thought that he was present 'only by grace'. How I have puzzled over this strange notion of grace! It seems that Teresa saw it as a sort of external stimulus from God, a sort of remote control. She seems not to have realised that grace involves presence. She learned it by experience.

For the reason that it brought me light when I was trying to work out Teresa's thought and experience, I will quote a passage from her collaborator, St John of the Cross. This passage, in my opinion, throws rare light on the nature of mysticism, showing what it really is:

> To understand the nature of this union, one should first know that God sustains every soul and dwells in it substantially... This union between God and creatures always exists. By it He conserves their being so that if the union would end they would be immediately annihilated.
>
> Consequently, in discussing union with God, we are not discussing the substantial union which is always existing, but the union and transformation of the soul in God. This union is not always existing, but we find it only where there is likeness of love. We will call it 'the union of likeness' and the former 'the essential or substantial union'. The union of likeness is supernatural, the other natural. The supernatural union exists, when God's will and the soul's are in conformity... It is true that God is ever present in the soul as we said, and thereby bestows and preserves its natural being by His sustaining presence. Yet He does not always communicate supernatural being to it. He communicates supernatural being only through love and grace, which not all souls possess. And those who do do not have it in the same degree.' The soul must labour to detach itself from itself so that 'God who is naturally communicating himself to it through nature may do so supernaturally through grace.'

'Grace' in this passage, is, for John, the mystical communication of God, which, although it is not actually given to all, is offered to all and will be given if only they will prepare to receive it. Referring to John 1.13, he explains that these words are fulfilled in 'those who, in their rebirth through grace and death to everything of the old man, rise above themselves to the supernatural and receive from God this rebirth and sonship which transcend everything imaginable. (*Ascent*, Bk 2 c V).

Teresa 'saw' this taking place, she 'saw' that the 'natural presence' of God sustaining our being, can become a presence of ineffable intimacy based on likeness. This growing likeness is an increased capacity and power to 'embrace' the God who is always offering himself, to 'know' him in a most intimate way. The 'centre' of the soul of which Teresa has, in this moment of grace become aware, is itself a *becoming*, a 'becoming-soul' or a 'soul-becoming'. It isn't so much that God is giving himself more – he is always giving himself fully – but that the soul *is* more and can receive him in a new way.

What must it be to 'see' God loving us? Is it any wonder that Teresa was ravished with joy? It does us good to read her outpourings, even to read of her psychic response provided we understand it, for it is not easy in our everyday lives, in our greyness and dryness, to keep our hearts aloft, to keep the mountain top before our eyes. We can go for encouragement and refreshment to the one who 'saw'. True, her own mode of expression, her choice of imagery may not appeal to us but at least we perceive the rapture of one who 'saw' in a similar way in which the apostles 'saw' the risen Lord. We can be inspired and encouraged without in any way desiring a like vision for 'blessed are they who have not seen and yet believe.' We must be absolutely convinced – and this commentary aims at establishing conviction – that exactly the same grace of intimacy is offered to us; we too can be totally transformed in love even in this life. 'Sight' such as Teresa had is given only to the few but when as in her case, she shares something of her sense of blinding Reality, we can happily accept the stimulation to our own faith and desire.

What we want to struggle with now is how we might express the identical grace Teresa is speaking of in 'light off' terms because this is what we need to understand. It is in this fifth mansion that Teresa faces squarely the question whether such 'favours' as the one she describes are essential to the union with God she is speaking of in the fifth mansion. She gives the unequivocal answer 'no'. At other times she is ambiguous as if uncertain; here she expresses herself quite clearly. We recall that this is her latest book, written towards the end of her life when her experience and thought had matured. Was it that she had actually encountered people of high spiritual quality yet lacking in these 'favours' who demonstrated the truth for her? Or was it an instinct of her own heart? She spells out for us how union can be obtained, 'by not following our own will but submitting it to whatever is the will of God'. This involves a 'dying' to ourselves.

Let us look carefully at her story of the silkworm. Her image of the castle is proving inadequate at this point, she needs a more dynamic one, of something that grows.

> When the warm weather comes, and the mulberry trees begin to show leaf, this seed [such she calls the egg] starts to take life; until it has this sustenance on which it feeds, it is as dead. The silk-worms feed on the mulberry leaves until they are full grown, when people put down twigs, upon which, with their tiny mouths, they start spinning silk, making themselves very tight little cocoons, in which they bury themselves. Then, finally, the worm which was large and ugly, comes right out of the cocoon a beautiful white butterfly . . . The silkworm is like the soul which takes life when, through the heat which comes from the Holy Spirit, it begins to make use of the general helps which God gives us all, such as frequent confessions, good books and sermons, for these are the remedies for a soul dead in negligences and sins, and frequently plunged into temptation. The soul begins to live and nourishes itself on this food, and on good meditations [second and third mansions] until it is full grown.

Generous effort in the first stages brings about a growth which allows something new to happen, a new stage in the evolution of the human being begins.

> When it is full grown . . . it starts to spin its silk and to build the house in which it is to die. This house may be understood to mean Christ. I think I heard or read somewhere that our life is hid in Christ, or in God . . . or that our life is Christ . . . His Majesty becomes our mansion as He is in this prayer of union, which, as it were, we ourselves spin.

What does she mean by the cocoon which we ourselves spin? She has clearly indicated that the grace she is speaking of is pure gift, a passive state of prayer, yet here she is saying we ourselves spin the cocoon, make the mansion which is Christ. Listen again – here is the very heart of the grace in question:

> That soul has now delivered itself into His hands and His great love has so subdued it that it neither knows nor desires anything save that God shall do with it what He wills. Never, I think, will God grant this favour save to a soul which He takes for His very own. His will is that, without understanding how, the soul shall go thence sealed with His seal.

Again she is wedding two things, an act of surrender on the part of the soul and a pure favour, something God does that seals the soul as his very own.

May I tell you about someone I know? If we align what she has told me with what we have just read of Teresa, I think we shall begin to perceive what it is all about. This person is 'light off'. God has brought her to a very close mystical union with himself. I asked her about this fifth mansion. What did she know of it? After all, she had never known an experience such as marked Teresa's fifth mansion, had she? No. But was there no experience *at all*? Could she say now, looking back, what her fifth mansion was? Her answer was that, looking back – the looking back is most important, she remembers the exact moment which she is sure *now* corresponds exactly with what Teresa says of her own experience, that is, in essence for there was no 'light on', no psychic repercussions. There was a 'moment', seemingly so poor and unobtrusive when she was given insight and a choice. In no sense whatever was there written over it 'Take note! This is God'. Far from it, it was, oh, so deeply hidden and yet now she sees it was a most powerful, creative grace, an invitation, a call. Recall the poetic expression of God's creative call summoning everything into being calling them to become something more; and, the creature that can consciously respond emerging, the 'Call' going on, hammering into his heart, summoning him to leave his animalistic

80

scabbard, then his humanistic one. This is what is happening now. There is a vibrant summons, full of power, calling the creature to transcend its material limits and shoot itself off to God. It is called upon to 'die' to itself, that is, to all it is of itself, and to consent to be taken away, right into the divine sphere. All that has gone before has been preparation for this. If you like, all that has gone before has been preparation for the firing of the rocket. The rocket had to be made and likewise the combustion to fire it. The 'moment' we are speaking of is the firing of the rocket and the rocket will infallibly reach its target. Once it is fired in this fashion nothing can stop it. If we change the metaphor we can say all that has gone before has been a preparation for knocking with one's whole being on the door and, infallibly, the door will open.

A divine and human work is involved. We can say it is a great human choice involving the whole person and of such resolution and power that *it gets there*; it is an *effective* determination. On the other hand we must say that such an act is beyond human capacity of itself; it posits a direct intervention of God, an infusion of divine energy. The graces we have called the fourth mansion are the beginning of the divine infusion fostering the growth of the soul. What Teresa calls the 'prayer of union' is the moment of definitive decision. Because through her 'light on' Teresa saw this happening, saw what God had accomplished in this moment, she felt it was a short cut; but it isn't really, no more than is the experience of 'light off'. When we read her *Life*, of the twenty years of her bitter struggle to give herself to God, and then come to the moment of her full conversion, the moment under discussion, we can hardly call it a short cut.

To go back to the person I know. Though in one sense she feels that from that decisive moment she had no choice (the light was so great, the impulse so strong that she could do no other) she knows objectively that this is not true – but again in a sense. Just because nothing happened on the psychic level it would have been easy to let it pass by and allow herself to take her place again in the world of reason and sense impressions, the world which seems so real to the 'natural man'. True, this grace

81

fell upon her with a sword of detachment in its hand. At one blow it severed some vital connection with ordinary reality. She was like Cain in reverse, branded with God's sign and an exile henceforth on earth. We shall never manage to distinguish clearly between the divine impulsion which seems to create a 'must' and the human activity of choice, consent. The two are intimately bound up with one another. Shall we say the human being is enabled to consent, enabled *not* to refuse what is yet bitter to nature? Yet we have to say that at the moment of offer, there is the possibility of refusal and perhaps we have to allow for the fact that some reach this point and then refuse. Is this what happened in Teresa's case? Did she mean that twenty years earlier she was brought to this moment of choice and shied off? Very, very much is being asked of flesh and blood, let us not forget, and the temptation to evade must be great indeed.

The person I know described to me how, for her, the crucial thing was just holding on to the insight she had been given at the time even though the impact of it had petered out. She knew she *had* seen the truth and that from henceforth her life must be governed by it. A torch had been put in her hand which she must keep on holding until she reached the end of a long, dark tunnel; a special kind of torch because its light was not visible to her. She just knew it had been put in her hand and that she must never let go of it, come what may. How many, many times she must have wanted to be rid of it, to abandon the bleak, lonely journey, to come out into the fresh air, see again the smiling fields and flowers. Was she sure she had a torch, anyway? Was it worth having? How did she know? Was the tunnel leading her any where? Was it *God's* way? What proof had she? Was it fantasy and illusion . . . that insight of so long ago? But on she went, never giving up not even for half an hour, always at it, as we would say, obsessed with her 'dream', suffering because she did not know she was loving God, because she saw herself ungenerous, with nothing about her to suggest that she was moving irresistibly towards her goal.

This is what it means in real life to be truly God's own, delivered into his hands, neither knowing nor desiring anything save that he should have what he wants. It does not mean that one never fails but it does mean that the compass is always set, the will stretched towards God without any slackening. This is the grace of the fifth mansion. It is not a mansion in the sense that it is a place where we are, it is a dynamic moment of decision, an invitation offered and accepted, understanding that this acceptance is beyond our power and is a direct effect of God's contact. Teresa talks of being put in one's own centre and by this she means that the person has emerged from its purely 'natural' state, though we must always remember this natural state is open to God, in his ambience and by 'natural' is meant what we are as material beings, what Paul means by 'flesh'. There is a 'centre' now which is spirit, and spirit means 'what is God's', what is being transformed into him, what is of his own being, a share in his divine nature, as we say. The response of the soul at this moment is of such a quality as to be impossible, inconceivable before this stage is reached. Given the mystic encounter of this mansion and the *response* of the soul, the rocket is shot, gathering momentum as it speeds along until it reaches its goal. The significance of this is *that we can have no knowledge of the fifth mansion until we can look back from the last, from the goal*. It can never be deduced from what we experience or have experienced, from what we feel or what we don't feel. We might think we want nothing but God and are surrendered to him. We cannot know whether this is true or not. The only way we know is *if we get there*. If we have really knocked, the door is opened, if we really have wanted God, we receive him whom we have wanted. Only *looking back* is it possible to discern that everything hung on a moment of grace though it might not be possible to put one's finger on the precise moment. This immediately shows the uselessness of wanting to know where we are on the spiritual journey. We cannot know, and what is more, to want to know is a self-seeking that cancels out wanting God alone which is characteristic of this stage.

Teresa recognises a definitiveness about the grace of union she is speaking of in the fifth mansion. It effects a transformation as great as that from a large ugly worm to a lovely white butterfly. We must note, however, that it is only a relative

83

transformation, it is not the transformation proper to the seventh mansion. The emphasis in the image of the butterfly is rather on freedom than on beauty. An old slavery has been cast off and there is freedom to speed towards God. The heavy weight of earthiness no longer pulls, now the new creature soars above the earth into another realm. It is not a question of a marvellous feeling of well-being such as follow on all sorts of thereapeutic activities and which facilitates right living, it is a question of *enablement* and this need not be accompanied by any emotion. It is a transformation of will not of feeling.

Yet there is ambiguity. Definitive? Yes. 'But we can be unfaithful', says Teresa. Clearly she is referring to herself but she does speak of others she has known, of 'great spirituality', who have fallen back. In the first place we must not think that this state of 'union' implies perfection, that everything is now done and that all we have to do is sit in the capsule as the rocket speeds along. This would be totally erroneous. It is a beginning of perfection, that is all. A long, long journey lies ahead involving great struggles. There will be falls, there will be some blindness for the soul is far from full maturity, yet, it seems to me, the very nature of this stage, what makes it precisely what it is, is the *definitiveness*, in that the momentum is never lost. Falls, failures are quickly repaired; the vital impulse is there to ensure this. 'Never, I think, will God grant this favour (of the prayer of union) save to the soul which He takes for His very own.'

It is the grace, I think, bestowed on Paul at his conversion, on the apostles after the resurrection of Jesus, whereby they became disciples in *very fact*. Judas to whom Teresa refers, was never a disciple of Jesus in this sense. It is the grace which baptism signifies and points towards but we have to say that rarely is it in operation.

When Teresa is bewailing failure she is, I think, referring to what comes before, either in not corresponding with the preparatory graces or, having been brought to the very threshold, refusing to cross it. We have to think of the fourth mansion in very diversified fashion. What is said there belongs sometimes to the very earliest grace of infused contemplation inviting us to leave the second or third mansions, but sometimes it refers to much more developed stages when we are being prepared for real conversion which will make us true disciples of Jesus and lights for the world. Teresa thinks Our Lord puts people through their paces, so to speak, testing if they can be relied on to use the big graces he wants to give for this purpose, and if they do not show the resolution necessary he will not give them, both for their own sakes – it would make their culpability very great – and for the sake of others.

She uses the image of betrothal. In Teresa's day betrothal was a serious step from which there was no retreat, it led infallibly to marriage. In the mansion we are speaking of, the soul is being tested and prepared. There has been preparatory discussion and exchange of gifts but now comes the Bridegroom's personal visit. From this an understanding grows. The soul now has some intimation not only of who he is but of what it is going to mean to have him as spouse. Will she accept or not? If the answer is yes, 'the contract is signed' and he grants her this definitive grace. The grace and the resolve it engenders are one thing as we have tried to explain. A number of people, we suggest, are brought to this choice but very few really surrender and go forward. Nevertheless, the graces these 'failures' have received are considerable and have had a marked effect. Such persons by now have a greater capacity for God and greater light and can give others light, Teresa thinks, provided they go on living good lives. She has, of course, her own experience in mind.

Once someone has really signed the contract, or shot her rocket something very momentous has happened in God's world. This person is going to have a profound influence in God's world and draw many along with her. This in no way implies that this influence or drawing is going to be apparent. It can happen and must happen at the deep springs of life; only here is the influence real. It is the awareness of the 'preciousness' of those who have got so far which sets Teresa's nerves on edge . . . how awful if they should fail; oh, they must be so diligent and watchful! But of course, they are, this watchfulness and diligence is part and parcel of the grace. It is worth noting, before we leave for a moment the ones who have leaped the gulf over into God's world in order to consider why the others do not get so far, to observe that, when recalling what she thought to be the 'prayer of union' in her youth, Teresa remarks 'it is true she had not yet experienced the effects which have been mentioned', and the sentence before, 'Later, the Lord gave her new Light'. In her introduction to the fifth mansion she affirms 'Some of the things which are in this room . . . are, I am sure . . . attained by very few'. These observations seem to me to add weight to the position held here that, though we must theoretically allow for failure (that is a real going back not just shortcomings and falls) in one brought so far, for no one can be wholly secure in this life, nevertheless, for all practical purposes this step, of its very nature, is an irrevocable one, and that we may conclude that the failures Teresa refers to belong to a preparatory stage; because the psychic experiences resounding from the mystical graces she received in the preparatory stage, seemed of the same kind as the one that actually set her in the fifth mansion, she was confused.

Addressing herself to her own spiritual family of Carmel, which, we must say, exists solely for the purpose of surrender to God in the profound way, under discussion 'few of us prepare ourselves for the Lord to reveal it to us, (the precious pearl of contemplation). This clearly shows that no external practices no matter how excellent in themselves, no matter how spiritually orientated, lead automatically to contemplation. Neither is it a question of severe austerities. No, what is involved is a searching interior mortification which few of us attempt to the degree necessary.' If you are to gain 'He would have you keep nothing back, whether it be little or much'. We have to spin our cocoon and this means we have to die to ourselves, 'renounce our self-love and self-will and attachment to earthly things.' We must practice penance, prayer, mortification, obedience and all the other good works we know of. There is nothing esoteric involved, no magical practices, nothing that lies outside our own every day life experience. It is a question of living the teaching of Jesus himself to the fullest degree; being wholly perfect as he said. 'Oh how many of us there are who say we do this and think we want nothing else, and would die for this truth'. It isn't enough to have entered religious life and to be living well. Watch for the pernicious worms which are always busy at their destructive work. Self-love again, self-esteem and censoriousness even in small matters and in subtle ways, and mediocrity in loving our neighbour. No question that we are not reasonably charitable – but where that outpouring of generous love and service such as Jesus shows us? 'We are so fond of ourselves and so very careful not to lose any of our rights'. No fear of self-squander! She proceeds to put the whole weight on love of the neighbour because, in practice, this is the way in which we love God. This is where she is so magnificent a guide, perhaps the more impressive now she is stressing practical charity, simply because she, personally *was* enamoured of 'experiences' and thought them important.

Her words seem to have a greater weight set against her appreciation of her 'favours'. Everything has to be set aside, she declares, when our neighbour is in need. She pokes at those who think union with God has to do with what we feel and who set themselves in their hidden corner, muffling themselves up lest their attention be diverted for a moment. Teresa was never really deceived. She knows by experience that we can get all sorts of 'religious' experiences if we go at it and really want them. But we do so at the cost of true values chief of which is devotion to our neighbour. We are too busy with our states of religious feeling to be bothered with him. And when we have attained them, of what value are they? Aware of the human tendency to place too much importance on our feelings she warns that abandonment to God's will and detachment do not rule out feelings of grief and sorrow in bereavement and so forth. These are natural movements and do not involve the will. Of course we see that our Lord suffered such feelings. The same tendency to interpret feelings as reality she warns us, leads to imagining we have virtues because we feel we have them. The only proof we have them is how we act in every day life. Are we humble when face to face with some humiliation. No amount of self-depreciation in thought, word or gesture is of any consequence, what matters is how we act when occasions present themselves.

If we were to offer advice to those who want to advance and to those who are spiritual guides, it would be to set the compass, so to speak; to aim at this gathering up of the self so as to be able to give that self to God. This has nothing to do with a psychic awareness, it happens in day to day life. It involves constant watchfulness for the call of God so as to answer with an immediate 'yes'. We miss countless opportunities when he is there offering himself because we don't notice him, we are not really looking for him. This is where our attention should be – the whole of it – on noticing where he is, what he is asking *now*, not on spiritual states, stages, what happens to us when we are at prayer, what we feel of God and all the rest of it. What matters is that at every moment of my life we are *there*, waiting, receptive.

Before leaving this mansion it is well to remark that, considering the hardships of 'light off' – Teresa herself draws attention to how hard it is to die and not to feel one is living a new life, to love without feeling one loves or that one is loved – we might be tempted to think that 'light on' has all the advantages; that life must be easier for them. This is a mistake. Teresa speaks of their trials being of a sublime nature and very severe. In more than one place in her writings she speaks of the cost of 'seeing'. So it is now. The 'light on' just because she 'sees' undergoes sufferings such as the rest of us cannot know. In some way they participate in our Lord's own experience of sin and rejection of love. Read what Teresa has to say of this unbearable torment. This is not mere emotionalism, it is the effect of 'seeing'. I am in the extraordinary position of being close to a 'light on' and, as an observer, know something of what happens and the toll token of the body. Here is a grief that ransacks mind and body. 'Light on' are called to give God a particular kind of love and compassion, not necessarily greater but of a kind that can only flow from 'seeing'.

For 'light off' as well as 'light on', the fifth mansion represents a union with Jesus in his death. That is the heart of it really, an effective resolution to enter into his sufferings and death.

One suffers in one way, the other in another. There is no short cut, no finding the work done for us. Each of us, if we would truly be Jesus' disciple must take up our cross and follow in his footsteps.

Sixth Mansion

The sixth mansion is a land of intimate communications of divine love, of vision, ecstasy, locution where we are admitted into the unspeakable riches of Christ, filled with spiritual knowledge and wisdom; a land too of suffering, for the wisdom is that of him who died and rose again; of experience of the power of his resurrection even as we share deeply in his death. There is a unity between the fifth, sixth and seventh mansions. The fifth ushers us into the contemplative life, the life of passionate love; the sixth is the living out of that love, the living of the surrendered heart; the seventh is the perfection of love. The grace of the fifth is the dynamism driving us forward, the sixth the actual journey, the seventh the goal reached. Here we see exemplified what God will do would we but let him.

> True though it is that these are things which the Lord gives to whom He wills, He would give them to us all if we loved Him as He loves us. For He desires nothing else but to have those to whom He may give them.

The decisive act of choice of the previous mansion opens us to God in a way not possible before, or, more accurately, so enlarges our capacity for him that he is able to give himself in an incomparably fuller measure. Thus his work now is full of power, and of infinite range of breadth and length and height and depth, surpassing all we could ask or think. The work of God in us now is consistent because we are consistent in our surrender. Hitherto we were not. For a short while, perhaps, we maintained an attitude of surrender and then our resolution waned and we abandoned it, falling again into self-protecting evasions of the loving pressures of God. Now it is different. All the time our heart is crying, 'come, Lord, do your will in me for I want nothing else'. This is what we see in Teresa. Here is one wounded with love, wanting his will so ardently that no price is too high – he must have everything, everything. And the divine answer is, 'and you, beloved, must have everything'. Inevitably as we move into these realms of intimacy, we take up the theme of marriage. In its highest expression, human marriage is the image of what takes place between God and the creature who chooses to belong to him. She has searched, she has laboured, she has knocked persistently and now she is beginning to find, the door is opening to her. Whether this betrothal, this irrevocable promise, 'I will be yours', and its certain response, 'I, always yours, will surely make you mine', takes place in 'light on' or 'light off' is irrelevant. The reality of betrothal is the same. Over and over again, regularly, consistently in ever increasing measure, divine Love bestows himself, without intermediary of any created, material thing. His vital, transforming embrace is, of its very nature, secret, unless it is his will to illuminate what is happening by a 'light on' experience which, it seems to me, must be described as supernatural in the strict sense. Otherwise it cannot be known directly. This unutterable work of God, let us call it a wooing, takes place in deepest darkness and secrecy. 'You are dead, and your life is hidden with Christ in God'. This life, hidden in God is our true life: now we have died to the life of 'flesh'. Bound as we still are in our mortal bonds we cannot see directly this new life, the life of the risen Lord, which is what we are living by; only in its effects do we know it. Faith tells us this is our inheritance, we have laboured to make it our own; we find ourselves profoundly changed and know that this is the work of God.

It will be readily surmised that the sixth mansion covers a very long journey. Figuratively, immense distances are traversed and, chronologically also, we can expect the journey to take a long time, consisting as it does of a total self-emptying, a dying to everything that is not God. It involves a tremendous growth and spiritual maturation far outstripping any natural maturation. Teresa's description of the sixth mansion gives the impression of one far advanced in it, someone on the threshold of the seventh, indeed she sees a door open between the two. If we have but the slightest intimation of our human selfishness we can surmise too that it will be a way of the cross. Teresa warns us of this. There will be sufferings from within and from without. 'Really, when I think of them, I am sometimes afraid that, if we realised their intensity beforehand, it would be difficult for us, naturally weak as we are, to muster determination enough to enable us to suffer them or resolution enough for enduring them.' She admits that, in order to endure what must be endured, some token is needed of 'this gain it now holds' – something of this life, 'hid with Christ', must be perceived, otherwise such trials could not be born. John of the Cross says similarly and it is probably universally true. It is impossible for us to have a desire strong enough to endure the purifying suffering preceeding transformation into God, without a divine impulse and divine strengthening. These, I think, are the grace of the fifth mansion. Again, it must be insisted, reality cannot be assessed by the intensity of conscious experience but by effectiveness – it impels us towards the goal. 'Light off' receives this impulse and fortitude every bit as really as 'light on', but they are 'hid', revealed only by what they effect. If the book of the Mansions itself is autobiographical, the chapters of the sixth mansion are supremely so. Here we have Teresa's own dramatic, high-powered, highly-coloured experience. Unless we keep this in mind we can get lost; we can give attention and importance to what is of so personal a nature as to be irrelevant for us, and the more so because, as we have said, and must continue to repeat, she, unlike ourselves, had 'light on' experience. Alongside this, she was a pronounced 'sensitive'. Her strong mystical life heightened her psychic powers and she could not distinguish between; one, her essential mystical grace; two, her 'light on' experience of it; and three, the vibrant echoes in her emotional and intellectual life. Thus, much of what we are shown in these chapters, is no more than paranormal phenomena, counterparts of which are by no means rare in contexts far removed from the truly mystical realm.

Not unconnected with her 'sensitive' nature and the crop of psychic experiences which sprang from it, is the rather dramatic nature of her trials. This vivid creature, abounding in nervous energy, who admits she was fond of the sensational (Way.c8) could ill endure monotony and drabness. Moreover, Teresa seems to have an unusually powerful need for security. In her day, and we ourselves are liable to the same notion, it was assumed that both extraordinary 'experiences' as well as extraordinary sufferings accompany a genuinely holy life. To have both of these seemed to give authentication. Unconsciously, this craving for security, could have had much to do with their occurrence in Teresa's life. Imagine the comfort and reassurance of hearing God calling you, 'beloved', or saying, 'fear not'! What a sense of specialness, security, it could afford! There is, of course, no question of saying Teresa made them up. To have done so would have been to depart from truth and effectively block God, which clearly Teresa did not. It is simply saying that she was a real, human person with a particular makeup, with good points and weak points. We are as we are and we go to God as we are, in the makeup we are. He is skilful in giving himself to us in what we are, through the makeup we are. Teresa was not a twentieth century woman, expected to know something of human psychology, She belonged to a different world, more credulous than our own. A few hundred years hence, those who come after us may look back and remark on how credulous we were in areas which seem to us carefully chartered! Our maintaining consistently that the mystical grace itself is most secret, means we have no difficulty whatever in allowing that God comes to us in every conceivable kind of experience, including our intellectual and psychic states. Once we have grasped that such experiences are *not* the mystical grace itself, are not God, not *directly* from him, but are to be classed with all the other ways he comes – through reading, good thoughts, people, events, and so forth – and that we can not be certain that they are the *effects* of mystical grace, then we can put aside all fear of illusion. Seen in this light, the torments Teresa endured on this score, her frenetic search for assurance of the genuineness of her experiences, were totally unnecessary. She could not have known this; we know it because of our modern knowledge of the workings of the psyche, and, above all, our knowledge of the existence of the unconscious. Leaving this aside, it is still difficult to understand how people could think that God is directly responsible for what causes such agonies of uncertainty. The path the gospel shows is not tortuous and ambiguous. God leads his children along straight paths.

What is truly marvellous in Teresa's life is not the 'marvellous' but the way everything served God's purpose, everything served love. What, in itself, could have been dangerous was turned into benefit and all because of her singleness of heart, because she really did want God. In the very area where, it seems, she was subtly seeking self – her craving for authenticating 'experiences', she met the purifying hand of God. For the measure of assurance afforded, there was meted out to her appalling anguish evoked by confessors and others who doubted their authenticity. With great vividness and pathos she describes the sheer torment of this doubt especially when it coincided with eclipses of her sun. She longed for the authoritative word, 'this is the work of God'. Often she heard, 'the devil', 'delusion': There was only one answer, and it is the only human answer to God whatever way he comes; that of utter trust and abandonment. This Teresa gave. One way or another, we must be brought to this total abandonment, this relinquishing of every security save that of the goodness and fidelity of God. It seems a roundabout way in Teresa's case but how marvellously skilful. Thus, he came to her in her phenomena, (*hers*, not his), and he came to her in her agony of doubt. When she tells us of this agony, it is hard to escape the conclusion that, deep down, she too had her own personal doubts. In spite of her delight in 'favours' she never lost a sense of truth. Over and over again she will reiterate that they are no certain sign of holiness, that there are holy people who have never seen a vision or heard a locution, and there are those who have who are far from holy.

'Light on' bears its own testimony within it. It cannot be doubted. Teresa herself observes this – certain experiences she cannot doubt. It is understandable that she is bewildered. On the one hand to be so certain, on the other, terrified that she is deluded. It is worth repeating that 'light on' has nothing to show for itself, so to speak. It escapes all categories of human expression and for this reason nothing can be said about it even to the self. But unless one understands how the psyche works, and how could Teresa be expected to do so, (we do not know *how* it works only that it does work), inevitably the conscious self wants to make something of it, is probably meant to do so; it wants to express it to itself. It is this 'externalisation' of the 'light on' revelation which can be written and spoken of, not the revelation itself. This I could not have known were it not that I have it from one who is 'light on'. She is a woman of intellect and academic weight and understands how it comes about that Teresa and others unconsciously seek to express in all sorts of mental and emotional experiences, what is, per se, inexpressible. Before looking at these love-enkindled expressions in the chapters ahead, there are one or two points of practical consequence to be considered.

This woman, 'wounded with love of the Spouse', seeks solitude. Anyone familiar with the life of Teresa will have some idea of the lax state of the convent of the Incarnation where she spent the first twenty years of her religious life. One of its chief defects was its worldliness, its disregard of the withdrawal, the silence and solitude to which it was bound by its rule. Once Teresa had undergone real conversion, she found herself totally dissatisfied with this state of affairs. Conscious of her weakness and need of safeguards, at the same time she yearns for a life of greater recollection, and this it was that inspired her to found the convent of St Joseph's and subsequent foundations. They were intended to be little deserts with opportunity for total exposure to God. We must not mistake her idea. Many times she warns us against escapism in the name of prayer, a seeking for a solitude which is nothing more than an escape from the conflicts, frustrations and burdens of life, nothing else than self-indulgence. For one 'wounded with love' this is unthinkable. Such a one knows experimentally that God is in the real human situation and *only there*, and that to live in solitude so as to be exposed to him, is to live in this real situation and shoulder these burdens, not cast them off.

On the charity of those who truly love this Lord and are aware of their own condition! How little rest will they be able to take if they see that they can do anything to help even one soul . . . How little real rest will they get out of any time they may rest in. (*Foundations*, 5)

How little solitude Teresa herself enjoyed from this time on. She was eaten alive by people and worn out with business. From looking at the life-style of her convents we get an idea of what she meant by living in solitude, being alone with the Alone. It is one directed to great purity of heart, to detachment from everything worldly, natural desires and ambitions. She did not establish an eremitical structure as she might have done, rather she established a community life with eremitcal elements, but with a spirit that is *totally* eremitical. Her nuns are called to be 'not merely nuns but hermits', detached from everything, totally exposed to God. Teresa grasped that, in order to be thus exposed one must be both purified and mature. For this we need others absolutely. There is no other means of purification than learning to live with others. It calls for continual sacrifice and provides opportunities for seeing the bad in us and for overcoming it. It keeps us wholly in touch with reality, coping with real people in real situations and this helps us to maturity. We could live in physical solitude and be exposed, not to God but to ourselves. We could remain immersed in selfishness, blind to our defects, undeveloped intellectually and emotionally. Is it ever allowed, I wonder, considering the absolute need we have of others, to take the initiative and choose the eremitical vocation? It could be presumptuous, a 'tempting God' in the old sense, expecting him to provide miraculously while we deliberately forego essential means to human and spiritual growth. The vocation to the purely eremitical life must, of necessity, be very rare, and, in my opinion, must in some way be forced upon us. Who of us would presume we were sufficiently purified and sufficiently mature on the personal level, to dispense with the society of others?

We hear that there is a revivial of the eremitical vocation today. I own to the greatest scepticism which experience only confirms. I am not referring to organised, semi-eremitical forms of life where there is the support and guidance of others, but even here, we have to beware of escapism, of the desire to feel very special and élitist. One of the most puzzling factors in the eremiticism or semi-eremiticism that has come my way, is how little actual time is given to unoccupied prayer, and yet one would have thought the raison d'etre of withdrawal, its only justification, was opportunity to spend many hours a day in prayer. Incidentally, it is worth mentioning here that the deeper our prayer, the more real it is and the more truly we are exposed to God in it, the less is it possible to spend long hours at it. It is literally impossible and if it were possible would be destructive. The pressure of God is too great. In my opinion, only someone endowed with 'light on', already sanctified, is fitted for the purely eremitical life, and even then, safeguards are needed and some social contacts.

If we have to remind ourselves that we must never give undue significance to 'favours' of whatever kind, the same must be born in mind regarding suffering. There can be an enormous amount of useless suffering that we really induce because we feel it to be authenticating, a sign that we are making progress, are specially close to God, a 'chosen soul' and so forth. We are wrong to attach such significance to suffering. All that matters any time, any where, is a strong, resolute cleaving to God, a determination to do his will, cost what it may. If suffering has a value it is only when it forces us to such acts of love. Of itself it is not sanctifying. As regards interior suffering for this is what is considered here, the only way to deal with it is to refuse to have it, refuse to suffer from it. We are far better off without it. If we can't get rid of it at will, we can use it by persistently lifting ourselves out of it, moving up into the real world of Truth and Love. This sort of inner suffering is fantasy, it has no reality. Reality is the life, the world, of the risen Jesus, where there is utter security and joy, where all is well and will be well. This is where we must live, not in our miserable subjective states of feeling, measuring life as seems to us, as we feel it to be instead of as it *is*. For many people, for us all, really, *the* surrender, *the* dying to self lies precisely here. It is not understood sufficiently. Masochism, dramatisation of suffering is every bit as common and just as much an obstacle as lack of generosity in bearing the hardships of life.

Teresa admits to having suffered grievous bodily infirmities for long, long years; she is scarcely ever without them and at times they are intolerable. She would much rather suffer martyrdom than these pains. It is the Lord, she thinks, who sends them. There is surely a connection between these physical pains and her psychic nature. She herself sees the connection between them and graces of prayer. In her earlier years, before she surrendered, the interior conflicts externalised themselves in excruciating pains which she bore with great patience. It is as if these physical tortures and the patient acceptance of them, were a substitute for the surrender she could not make. This desperate state of acute and prolonged pain in which she felt 'decomposed' and at her wits ends, were another area for abandonment and trust. All things work for good to those who really want God, really love him. Most of her bodily illnesses were of psychosomatic origin, as is clear. It has already been noted that the 'light on' experiences tends to result in a physical weakening – the pressure on the person is very intense for it is not a natural way of experiencing God.

One accustomed to 'light on' must find its obscuration extremely painful; likewise, one accustomed to psychic responses must feel desolate when, for some reason or another, they fail to occur. Teresa describes states of aridity in her usual high tones. Those of us for whom they are daily bread will not feel them in the same way. Nevertheless, it must never be a case of just putting up with aridity, we have to use it to grow in faith and trust and disregard for self. To live for long years in aridity, accepting it with love and confidence effects a thorough self-emptying; it is pure love. For one in the sixth mansion, be they 'light on' or 'light off', because God is so very close and he is a purifying, transforming fire, there will be deep suffering. The advice remains the same as that above when non-mystical suffering was in question. We must refuse to suffer from it, we must keep leaping up into the world of light, security and joy.

We must now see what can be usefully said of the favours

Teresa treats of in the following chapters. Possibly what can be said of nearly all of them:- 'influences so delicate and subtle that they proceed from the very depth of the heart' and enkindle fire (c 2); the certain consciousness of the presence of the Spouse (c 2); rapture (c 4); flight of the spirit (c 5); prayer of jubilation (c 6); intellectual visions (c 8); impetuous transports of love (c 11), is that the foundation of them is a profound embrace of divine Love, actually 'seen' by the 'light on' faculty. Now in one way, now in another, Teresa's highly sensitised psyche reacts. Often, she is unconsciously dramatising the inner grace. In rapture, for instance. The very essence of the sixth mansion is rapture, the wrenching of the self away from its self. Each mystical encounter momentarily effects this whether it be seen or not, until love and desire are so intense that the self chooses to surrender totally once and for ever. The psychic phenomenon Teresa describes as rapture, acts out this inner event. It is not without value for us. It helps us to understand what God does. At the same time it must be clear how unimportant in itself, in spiritual significance, is this little drama. What matters is the actual surrender taking place in secrecy. 'God's will seems to be to show the soul that, since it has so often and so unconditionally placed itself in his hands, and has offered itself to Him with such complete willingness, it must realise it is no longer its own mistress . . .' Teresa remarks how much courage, faith, confidence and resignation are required to undergo rapture. Utterly true is this of the only rapture that counts, that of allowing oneself to be taken away from oneself so as to live in God. Rapture, flight of the spirit, as described by Teresa as phenomena, are not confined to the truly mystical realm. We can hear of them, read of them happening in wholly secular, humanistic, even evil contexts.

A quotation from Colin Wilson's book *Mysteries* will have great significance in our context principally because the experience described – it is that of a modern Yogist – so closely resembles what St Teresa considered one of her most sublime experiences, the flight of the spirit.

During one such spell of intense concentration I suddenly

felt a strange sensation below the base of the spine, at the place touching the seat. The sensation was so extraordinary and so pleasing that my attention was forcibly drawn down towards it. The moment my attention was thus unexpectedly withdrawn from the point at which it was focussed, the sensation ceased... When completely immersed I again experienced the sensation, but this time, instead of allowing my mind to leave the point where I had fixed it, I maintained a reigidity of attention throughout. The sensation again extended upwards, growing in intensity and I found myself wavering; but with great effort I kept my attention centred round the lotus. Suddenly with a roar like that of a waterfall, I felt a stream of liquid light entering my brain through the spinal cord... The illumination grew brighter and brighter, the roaring louder, I experienced a rocking sensation and then felt myself slipping out of my body entirely enveloped in a halo of light... I felt the point of consciousness that was myself growing wider, surrounded by waves of light. It grew wider and wider, spreading outward, while the body, normally the immediate object of its perception, appeared to have receded into the distance until I became entirely unconscious of it. I was now all consciousness without any outline, immersed in a sea of light, simultaneously conscious and aware at every point, spread out, as it were, in all directions without any barrier of material obstruction. I was no longer myself, or, to be more accurate, no longer as I knew myself to be, but instead was a vast circle of consciousness in which the body was but a point, bathed in light and in a state of exaltation and happiness impossible to describe.

And another similar experience:

First there is the indescribable sensation in the spine as of *something mounting up*... This was accompanied by an extraordinary feeling of bodily lightness, of well-being, of effortlessness... It was also, somehow, a feeling of living more in the upper part of one's body than in the lower.

The yogist speaks of the chakras or power-points and that the desire for God involves the highest chakras in the crown of the head. All of which was known experimentally by Teresa but is it to be wondered at that she did not understand its physical nature?

100

It is characteristic of Teresa's 'experiences' that they were all weighted with knowledge, communicating 'certain truths concerning the greatness of God'; 'light and knowledge of His Majesty'; 'some part of the kingdom she has won by being His'; 'she learns so many things at once'; 'great things are shown to the soul' . . . we could continue. Teresa is sure that this inner content is one of the essential proofs of the genuiness of such 'experiences'. If they are empty, leaving nothing behind, they are not from God, she argues. The first and most important thing to note is that every mystical encounter, since it is a direct contact with God, is a communication of light, of knowledge; not an intellectual, theoretical knowledge, but a living knowledge that translates itself into holy living. Unless we can witness this growth in living wisdom we have no criterion of the presence of the mystical. The knowledge is essentially that of how to live so as to please God, the ability to recognise him however he shows himself – a knowledge of his ways, and likewise, a knowledge of his holiness, love and beauty, perhaps most secret to the conscious self, which reveals the self to the self in its ugly sinfulness, and of this it is vividly conscious. It causes great pain. Teresa refers to it many times in this sixth mansion: confusion at her ingratitude, lack of generosity, a growing contempt for self and a realisation that one is the least of all. Without this growing self-knowledge and humility we have no evidence of the mystical.

In the case of 'light on', the infusion of knowledge is more experiential though, as said, 'light on' in itself, escapes formulation. (Teresa makes the point that there are some experiences about which she can say absolutely nothing) However, 'light on' can be focussed on particular data, and it would seem this is what Teresa is referring to sometimes, in chapter 10, for instance, where it is revealed to the soul how all things are seen in God, and how within Himself He contains them all; again,

It may also happen that, very suddenly, and in a way which cannot be described, God will reveal a truth that is in Himself and that makes any truth found in creatures seem like thick darkness: He will also manifest very clearly that He alone is truth and cannot lie.

That these insights had their origin in a true mystical experience is proved by their effects:

> I mean that we must walk in truth, in the presence of God and man, in every way possible to us. In particular we must not desire to be reputed better than we are and in all we do we must attribute to God what is His, and to ourselves what is ours, and try to seek after truth in everything.

Her first daughters bear witness to her concern for truth in word and deed; it was a thing she impressed deeply on them. And then we have her humility which is, perhaps, the most outstanding thing about, her, a humility born of Light's proximity and his particular manifestations.

It would seem that at least great insight into spiritual matters, luminous intuitions into reality, would be sure signs of true mystical experience. It is not so. What Teresa describes of her intellectual vision of Truth itself and how all things are in God, find echoes in literature. We could quote examples of this and similar insights that are the product of keen minds and highly developed sensibilities; they are not uncommon with the 'sensitives'. Likewise, among theologians and biblical exegetes, we meet insights of such profundity and truth as to overwhelm us. These again need not indicate close union with God. Teresa herself was aware of this. She went to men of learning and used their insights well aware that they were not, as she would say, 'spiritual'. There is simply no certain criterion for the presence of the mystical save holiness of life. All the same, there *is* a knowledge, wisdom, insight, that is exclusive to the mystic. If expressed it would only be so in the same concepts others use. The difference lies in its 'livingness', in its permeation of the person. The mystic knows it as others do not, even though others say the same thing. Only another mystic can pick up the resonances, can enter into this living experience of God. In a sense, the knowledge, the experience *is* them, it is their own reality, the fabric of their being. Whether they ever express it even to themselves, is irrelevant. It is the knowledge Jesus speaks of: 'In that day you will *know*'; 'I will reveal myself to him'; 'In that day you will *see* me because I live and you also shall *live.*' The mystic is living by the life of Jesus and knows him in the intimacy of love. Rightly it was said at the beginning of this chapter, that the sixth mansion is essentially a land of vision and of rapture.

In this land also locutions abound; not precisely in the sense Teresa describes, but essentially. Here we hear secrets no tongue can utter. God speaks to us, in our inmost hearts. His words now are engraven in our hearts, not merely heard with the ears, read, understood intellectually. Teresa spends a lot of time discussing the phenomenon of locutions which, she declares, is common among prayerful people. She discerns three possible sources: God, our own imagination, the devil. We need not spend long on the subject. What has been said of visions applies in great part to locutions. God makes use of these natural phenomenon, whether they are, more consciously, the fruit of our wishful thinking: ourselves more or less consciously answering ourselves; or whether they arise from the unconscious. It is these latter that Teresa mistakes as coming directly from God. The unconscious can produce the impression of great authority, Teresa speaks of. It can also, in some mysterious way, actually foresee what will happen – what greater proof of their divine origin! (Teresa tactfully omits the occasions, of which we have witness, when 'God' told her of what was to happen but which failed to happen). To one who knew nothing of the unconscious, they must have been an extraordinary, supernatural happening:

> the soul has not been thinking of what it hears – I mean the voice comes unexpectedly . . . often it refers to things which one never thought would or could happen, so that the imagination could not possibly have invented them, and the soul cannot be deceived about things it has not desired or wished for or that have never been brought to its notice.

Let us, for a moment, put ourselves in Teresa's context and that of her nuns, many of whom seem to have been illiterate. Relatively speaking, Teresa was educated, but what chance had she or any of them, of a sound theological education? What chance had they of a knowledge of scripture? Vernacular versions of the bible were not available. The liturgy, intended to be the table of holy scripture spread before us daily for our nourishment, was in a language they could not understand. Teresa's quotations from scripture were often, it seems, picked up from books of devotion she read where she met them in the vernacular. To crown all, even some books of devotion were proscribed for them. Where could these poor women find nourishment for their spiritual lives. Sermons, converse with 'learned men', direction from confessors largely. No wonder Teresa was full of anxiety that her nuns had liberty to consult a variety of priests and that these should be learned men. She sought out the latter with passionate solicitude. But is it any wonder that these starved women, in their desire for God, craved for assurances, craved to *know*, wanted and induced revelations, locutions – tokens of God's care and love. What it must have meant for them to have been granted a vision, a locution, that bore all the marks of authenticity! What comfort, what assurance! It is indicative of Teresa's utter purity of heart and abandonment that even in such circumstances, she would affirm persistently that one could never stand by them, never take total security in them. What counted and counted only was growth in virtue. If this principle is firmly held, then what matter when such 'favours' abound! Even if they are the product of our imaginations, if they help us to love God more, to find comfort in him, if they make us more aware of our lowliness, why not be grateful? Why worry? Such her practical advice.

> The greater the favour the soul receives, the less by far it esteems itself, the more keenly it remembers its sins, the more forgetful is it of its own interest, the more fervent are the efforts of the will and memory in seeking nothing but the honour of God rather than being mindful of its own profit, and the greater is its fear of departing in the least from the will of God.

This growing disregard of self is the most striking characteristics of the sixth mansion, the opposite side of the coin to passionate, obsessive love for God.

Think now of our own situation. Daily we feed on the word of God, at Mass, at the Office. Vernacular translations of scripture are at our disposal. Moreover, we have a mine of biblical scholarship to explore if we take the trouble, all means of enriching us with truth, with a knowledge of God in his Jesus. It would surely be frivolous of us to be wanting the assurances, the revelations which supported Teresa and her contemporaries. The desire could spring from laziness. We don't want the hard work of searching for this knowledge for ourselves, we would rather have it without labour. It could mean that we were wanting, not God, but a desire to feel very special. We have all the assurance we need in holy scripture, in the sacraments at our disposal. These thunder in our ears and in our hearts if we would let them, that God loves us, that he will do everything for us, that everything is mine and all for me for Christ is mine and all for me. But not a bit of it. That's common, that's for everybody. I want that special word, special food, not the common meal. All such selfish desires, which lurk in the hearts of each of us, though manifesting themselves in different ways, have to be completely anihilated if we would be united to God. Disregard of self, total disregard of self, is the other side of union with God. We must die in order to live the only true life. On the other hand, there are those of us who have a psychic make-up, and a genuine spiritual life burgeons in psychic experiences of one kind or another. Provided we grasp that they are *ours*, from us and not from God, there is no reason why we should not profit by them as we profit by everything else.

In our situation also, we can hardly need the dependance on spiritual direction. This can be harmful. It can be a shirking of hard work, a shirking of responsibility. It can also be a craving to be special not just an 'ordinary Christian'. Perhaps we want a spiritual admirer, a flattering mirror reflecting back to us the image we would like to have, of being 'a rare soul', 'a contemplative'. Understandably we want reassurances about the way we pray, the value of our prayer. This we can never have. No one can give it to us for there are no ways it can be assessed. That is, no account we give of it is of any importance. With the best will in the world, the best of directors can misread what is

105

said or written and can do more harm than good. The best form of direction, and the only one we need – I am referring specifically to our way of praying – is the opinion of those we live with. Let us listen to them, to their assessment of our lives. Here we find the only answer. Let it not be our admirers but those we can trust to be objective or even those who dislike us. They can usually indicate areas of weakness and selfishness! These tell us of the nature of our prayer.

We have yet to discuss chapter 7. Deliberately it has been left to the end in order to give it the importance it deserves. Almost never is Teresa consistent in dealing exclusively with the stage she sets out on. One idea suggests another and without hesitation she discusses whatever seems useful regardless of order. Thus much of what she writes about in the sixth mansion does not refer to this stage but to earlier ones. This is particularly true of chapter 7. There are two points closely related: a warning against 'angelism', and insistence on the indispensable role of the 'Sacred Humanity' in our spiritual life.

Speaking rather generally of those who have made some progress, who seem to have received some mystical grace, she observes that one of the effects of this is to make discursive meditation impossible. She admits the validity of this difficulty but strongly deprecates any supposition that this rules out every form of meditation. We must remember that in her days Ignatian spirituality had an enormous impact; she herself was directed by Jesuits and affirms what great help they gave her in the life of prayer. No doubt at this time, the Ignatian form of meditation was well understood and did not suffer from the misconceptions later to be built around it. Certainly, in their direction of her, the Jesuits showed a remarkable flexibility regarding the method of meditation. Teresa's own way of teaching prayer to her novices was influenced by this tutelage. She insists here, as she has insisted earlier, that there can be no question of us mortals reaching a point of 'spirituality' where we no longer need to use our minds, where we can, at will, soar to heights of formless prayer. We are men, not angels, she says. It seems that in Teresa's day there was considerable controversy around this subject. Is it true only of her times? Is it not a perennial itch? It has to do with human pride. Secretly we want to be 'soul' not body and we imagine that progress in spirituality means living in some sort of 'spiritual' world where everything must be very different from what it is now; our interior experience must surely undergo a transformation from gosling ungainliness to swanlike grace. If from time to time we have had some sort of experience of enchanting newness – how marvellous it is – we crave to receive it again. We feel sure that this is the *real* thing, what the spiritual life is all about even though our well-instructed minds tell us differently. We long to establish this feeling as a permanent state. But we have no guarantee, have we, that this feast was spiritual in the true sense, and anyway, it is selfish to covet its return.

We have got it into our heads and many books encourage the notion, that it is more advanced and spiritual to give up thought and reflection – to say that we can't 'do it'; that it is much more contemplative to remain with blank minds waiting for God to act. Teresa is adamant: it is sheer waste of time. What is more, it is pride, a refusal to be human. Much has already been said on this in the fourth mansion. Ten years earlier, in the *Life*, she discusses it with the same insistence. Obviously she sees it as of paramount importance and begs us to believe her against everyone who would give different advice.

This question leads on naturally to the necessity for continual reflection on our Lord's life and death. Again, in spite of accurate theological knowledge of his absolute and unique mediatorship, in practice, many of us have the secret notion that we are working to get beyond this to a 'pure' prayer where 'God' is experienced directly, where we no longer need Jesus. We are failing to see the import of Jesus' words that to see him is to see the Father, that to know him is to know the Father, that to be in him is to be in the Father and that we have no direct link with the Father, if by 'direct' we mean other than through Jesus. We want to think we have but we have not. 'No one can come to the Father but by me', and this, not in the sense that you use me to get to him and when you have got to him you don't need me anymore, but you have simply no contact with the Father except through me in time and in eternity. But of

107

course, this *is* direct contact. Jesus' communication *is* 'pure God' and only his communication is 'pure God'. What we call the mystical, a direct, unmediated contact with God, *is* Jesus. He is his living touch. We have this direct contact only in him. Now, one advanced in the mystical way knows this. Teresa has no need to exhort *them* not to forget that Jesus is the source of all their good. He is becoming their life and they know it. He *is* their prayer, their union with God. The fundamental grace of entry into the mystical states is that Jesus becomes our Jesus. We begin to grope into the fathomless caverns of Jesus. We realise we never knew him before. We see life, reality everything in terms of him. His is the face always present in our consciousness as his life is secretly, escaping our consciousness, substituting itself for ours. We are becoming Jesus. No question about it but that there will be sheer avidity to know all we can of him, to seek the linaments of his beloved face in the gospels, and always we shall find him more and more. What we understand and know we understand will be more than we can bear, but more important still is his own wisdom infused into depths we cannot see.

If this sixth mansion is the land of vision it is essentially the vision of Jesus who in himself reveals the Father and puts us in the Father's heart; If there are secret words, they are secrets of the Incarnate Word. If there is rapture, it is this surrendered One catching us up in his own surrender to the Father. Jesus *is* surrender, and what he shows us, what he enables us to do, is to surrender also. We have no other objective in this life; it is the fulfilment of our nature to effect this surrender. We are only human when we have completely forsaken ourselves in love. The other side of fulfilment – the Father's answer – is not our business. Our whole intent as Jesus' was must be to surrender no matter what the cost. We are absolutely certain as he was of ultimate fulfilment because of his Father's love. He trusted his Father, he did not seek to peer into the future to see the form of this fulfilment; he was too absorbed, too in love to look beyond his present task of surrender. In this mansion Jesus is effecting his own surrender in us, drawing us away from all self-interest, making his love ours. It is a profound sharing in his death, but a death that is only the reverse of life. Way, Truth and Life – comprehensive terms. He is simply everything for us. But note, these words are put on the lips not of the risen Lord but of the earthly Jesus when he stood on the brink of his awful passion. The earthly Jesus whom John shows us as troubled, distraught, overflowing with tears. He is the Way precisely as this 'poor' one, experiencing the weight of human emptiness and incompletion. As such he is Truth, as such he is Life. And we fancy things should be different for us! Most of our anxieties stem from this error. We can't accept and be happy and content in this 'poor' experience. We can't see that this, embraced with love, *is* union with God. It is to be in the Way who is always *there* in the heart of God.

With the close of the sixth mansion we leave this obsessed, enamoured creature, ravaged with desire, a hungry emptiness nothing can satisfy. God has enlarged her capacity to infinite depth but they are not yet filled. She is still incomplete. Nothing she can do can effect the final act of rapture which takes her out of herself into him. 'Suspended', as Teresa says, she can only hang meaningless until it is effected. It is the total acceptance of this total dependency, together with total trust that God will act, which allows God, with a mighty sweep to carry her off as his prey.

Seventh Mansion

There is a disconcerting flatness about the seventh mansion, a sense of anti-climax. Is Teresa tired? Has she lost interest in her treatise but knows she must press on and complete it? These chapters lack the verve characteristic of her writing. The reason is simply that *there is nothing that can be said about the seventh mansion.* Entering into it we are in a world where human words are meaningless. Teresa feels this instinctively. She must say something, she takes up her pen and gropes for words, realises that what she has said is banal, useless, tries again and again, meandering on, getting nowhere. There is nothing here that she has not already said yet she knows that what she is now talking about is utterly different from everything that has gone before. But what is she to do? What can she say? Is there any point in saying anything? As our task is to expound Teresa's writing, we too must press on in her footsteps, groping as she does but all the time with a sense of complete futility if not of the ridiculous.

'We know that when he appears we shall be like him for we shall see him as he really is' (1 John 3:2). The seventh mansion is this vision of Jesus; not an intellectual insight but a transforming union. The seventh mansion *is* Jesus, he living in us and we in him, the perfection of marriage. After this there is really no more to be said. 'Tranquilly and noiselessly, does the Lord teach the soul in this state, he and the soul alone have fruition of each other in the deepest silence'. All that is possible of description is the self: what the self sees, understands, feels, does. Here the self is lost and there is nothing any more to talk about. But we must turn to Teresa's text and try to follow her.

Characteristically, Teresa expresses to herself and us what the seventh mansion is in terms of visions. This is her own medium for her deepest experience; she can use no other. She is certain now that she is 'endowed with life by God'; that it is by his own life that she lives. Her intimacy with him is now completely independent of the faculties. Somehow everything is taking place in her deepest centre inaccessible to all but God. This is, she understands, the fulfilment of what Jesus promised, 'that He and the Father and the Holy Spirit will come to dwell with the soul which loves Him and keeps His commandments'. Through her mysterious 'light on' faculty she sees the truth of this threefold relationship within herself and exclaims, 'Oh, God help me'! What a difference there is between hearing and believing these words and being led in this way to realize how true they are'. Unconsciously her psyche produces a mental image in conformity with her ready-made concept of 'Trinity'. This image is not the least important, we must remember that what is happening and what she sees is happening is quite *ineffable*.

Then she enjoys another vision, significantly after receiving Communion. It is of Jesus, the 'Sacred Humanity' as she likes to distinguish. He is the partner in the marriage. Her union is with him and it is through him in the Spirit that she has fellowship with the Father. This is the crucial insight. Now is realized what is meant by Christ being our life and that only in him are we in the Father. But again she wants to impress on us that this vision is quite, quite different from anything that has gone before. After all, this is not the only vision she recounts of the Sacred Humanity. Yet it is so different, belonging to another world. She cannot express the difference but different it is. Any seeming likeness is due to the fact that she has to use words and words are quite incapable of defining mystery, they can only suggest it. The essence of this vision is a transference of life. Teresa must be totally concerned henceforth with Christ's interests leaving hers in his care. A bridal-theme. A great self-forgetfulness envelops her.

Perhaps when St Paul says: 'He who is joined to God becomes one spirit with Him' [Phil 1:21], he is referring to this sovereign Marriage, which presupposes the entrance of

111

His Majesty into the soul by union . . . in those already prepared to put away from them everything corporeal and to
leave the soul in a state of pure spirituality; so that it might be
joined with Uncreated Spirit in this celestial union. For it is
quite certain that, when we empty ourselves of all that is creature and rid ourselves of it for the love of God, that same
Lord will fill our souls with Himself.

By choosing to open ourselves to God, to obey the summons to
life more abundant, uncoiling from our self-centred embryonic
state, we become what we are, what we are meant to be, 'He
destined us in love to be his sons through Jesus Christ . . . to
know the love of Christ which surpasses knowledge, that you
may be filled with all the fulness of God' (Eph. 1:5; 3:19). God
infallibly gives himself to the waiting openness and in this gift
we become ourselves. God gives himself to all that is; the
measure of their being is the measure of his gift, but only man,
of all the creatures known to us, can freely receive and respond
to this self-bestowal of God. He alone can receive God 'directly' in a 'personal' exchange, what we call intimacy, friendship,
love. And it is only when God has been able to love us in fulness
that we are wholly *there*. Only that in us which is divine is real.
Only when we are God-filled are we truly human. This is man's
meaning and destiny, finding its summit and archetype in
Jesus. This is the state of 'pure spirituality' Teresa is speaking
of, when all we are is transformed into God, when nothing of
the self remains in possession. She is not suggesting what we
attain in this life a state of immateriality, becoming 'angelic'.
 Teresa expresses this truth in her own terms of entering the
castle of the soul. Here the inmost chamber is reached at last;
the centre where the king makes his permanent abode. 'He
introduces her into His own mansion', 'the soul always has her
God in her inmost centre'. It is no longer a question of a passing
contact with the king dwelling in the centre; this is mutual and
permanent abiding, Lover in the beloved. There can be such an
abiding only when the full potentiality of the creature has been
realized, by God communicating himself to it and the creature
responding in love and surrender. Thus the inmost room is
nothing but the full growth of the creature. This mansion is no

staging inn but the end of the long journey; it is home. 'I will come again and take you to myself so that where I am you may be with me'. (John 14:3.)

In her futile attempt to explain the difference between this seventh mansion and those preceeding it she compares the bringing together of two candle flames. Momentarily the two are one, wax, wick, flame. But they can be separated. This is like the transitory union of the sixth mansion. Whereas the union now in question is indissoluble as raindrops falling into the river, the streamlets flowing into the sea are totally lost.

An outstanding feature of this state is its security. Teresa hardly knows herself, she who all her life-long has been plagued with insecurity, torn with anxiety. It is as if she can hardly accept her present security and looks around anxiously for snags. Perhaps it is a lack of humility to feel so secure; if this is so then it cancels out the possibility of union, doesn't it? So she makes an effort to put things right, to modify her assertion of total safety. She states the obvious. We are safe only insofar as we stay in God's hand. Separated from him we are capable of any fall. But the whole point of the matter is that now we cannot escape from God's hand. Our choice has been irrevocably made and his fidelity is absolute. In a real sense we have become him and he has become us. We find this timidity and hesitancy all through these chapters. In her heart Teresa knows she is utterly safe and can never be separated from God, that she is at home for ever. What unspeakable security to know that all is accomplished, the struggle is over, the end attained definitively! But she dare not say so, even to herself. We have a letter, written four years later, just one year before her death, to an old friend. We still hear overtones of Teresa's endemic anxiety, but she expresses herself more assuredly and is not afraid of saying just what she feels like. The letter is interesting in that it is saying the same things as she says here in the *Interior Castle* but we detect a greater freedom, confidence and abandonment. It seems as if this mansion held surprises for Teresa. She is perfectly happy and contented but she can't wholly adjust her preconceived ideas to cope with it. Some of her most cherished notions of what a fervent spiritual life is all about are overturned.

> Oh, if only I could give Your Lordship a clear idea of the
> quiet and calm in which my soul finds itself! For it is now so
> certain that it will have the fruition of God that it seems to be
> now in possession of it already, though it is not yet enjoying
> it. (*Relation* VI)

Not only does she no longer suffer suspension and ecstasy, but
she has lost her passionate grief at the 'loss of souls'. Her ardent
desire for heaven, her passionate desire to suffer. This absence
of suffering can make her uneasy. Over and over again Teresa
has expressed to us her conviction that great sufferings are a
prerequisite for great love; the measure of our love is the
measure of the suffering we can bear. She must keep on assuring herself that she is ready to suffer. At the same time she sees
that it is not suffering that is important at all! She tells us that she
cannot really suffer any more because she is no longer lonely,
she is enjoying continually divine companionship. Lest we mis-
understand her she goes on to tell us that she suffers very much,
and, indeed, we have external witness for the fact. The years
following the mystical marriage were for her fraught with difficulties of all kinds. Her letters bear witness to them and the
testimony of eye-witnesses. Again, it is all part of that ineffable
difference she cannot get across to us. She suffers but she
doesn't suffer! A sort of 'deadness' takes over, bewildering
indeed to this passionate woman, so used to a spiritual life of
emotional ardours.

> Hence comes the fear which sometimes haunts me, though
> without the disquiet and distress which formerly ac-
> companied it, that my soul has sunk into stupor, and that,
> because I cannot do penance I am accomplishing nothing.
> My acts of desire for suffering and martyrdom and the vision
> of God that I make have no strength in them and as a rule I am
> unable to make them at all. I seem to be living simply for the
> sake of eating and sleeping and avoiding any kind of distress;
> and even this does not distress me, except that sometimes, as
> I say, I am afraid of being deluded. (*Relation* VI)

The security Teresa enjoys destroys any need for impressive, reassuring ardours, visions, raptures. All these things are a product of the self, the self impressing itself, assuring itself that it is loving God, doing something for God. There is no need for this now. The self is dead to self, it lives in God, he does all. Hence the sense of apathy, low-keyedness, non-experience. Yet 'I believe that no strong attachment to any creature or to all the glory of heaven has any dominion over me. My one attachment is to the love of God, and this has not been diminishing'. (*Relation* vi).

Teresa observes a self-forgetfulness which is so complete that it really seems as though the soul no longer existed, because it is such that she has neither knowledge nor remembrance that there is either heaven or life or honour for her, so entirely is she employed in seeking the honour of God'. Yet the 'forgetfulness' is deeper than she can observe; it is loss of self not merely forgetfulness of self. It can best be expressed in the profound sayings John puts on the lips of Jesus. Jesus expressly declares that he has nothing of himself: the works he does are not his but his Father's; the judgments he makes are dictated by the Father; the whole initiative of his life derives from the Father. He exists as a sort of emptiness through which the Father speaks and acts. At the same time, paradoxically, he exists as a highly individual man firm in decision, act and judgment. There is nothing cipher-like in his personality. This is the mystery: man is that being who only becomes himself when he has surrendered totally to God; only when he is lost to himself is he fully *there*. Jesus experienced himself as having no life of his own, no power, no wisdom. All these he derived from his Father. On our side, we derive all from Jesus. As the Father is his life, so Jesus is ours and thus the Father is ours. One with Jesus we live with him in the Father, from the Father. We must not think for a moment that transformation into Jesus robs a person of individuality, that from henceforth they have no emotions, no preferences, no interests. Transformation into Jesus means we become fully human.

In this inadequate commentary on Teresa's seventh mansion we have avoided making a distinction between the experience of 'light on' and 'light off'. As we have followed her text we have been looking at a 'light on' but all that we have said so far applies equally to 'light off'; the same fundamental happening, the same self-loss and absolute security in a world inexpressible. To go further in an attempt to describe or distinguish would lead to unreality. As we read through Teresa's own effort to tell us of her own experience we sense the confusion into which she runs; how rash then to speak of what might or might not be. What has been said here seems to be all that can reasonably and safely be said.

Both Teresa and John of the Cross have attempted the impossible in describing the land of transforming union. We run the risk of taking them literally, of thinking that they are saying it is really like this; this happens, that happens, whereas what they are doing is trying to find imagery, words, for what is outside the range of words. It is 'what eye hath not seen, ear heard nor the heart of man has conceived'. When the summit of the mountain is reached what is there to describe? Nothing but sky. What can be seen and talked about are the pathways up the mountain. From the vantage point of the summit these can be seen in their fascinating detail. Thus we can never describe where we are on the spiritual ascent but only where we have been. When the top is reached we can say nothing about it nor is there any 'further on' from whence we may look back and see what it was like. The mountain top, the seventh mansion can be seen only from heaven for it really belongs there. Thus we leave Teresa in profound contentment: 'to this wounded hart are given waters in abundance. Here the soul delights in the tabernacle of God'.

Conclusion

'I came to cast fire upon the earth; and would that it were already kindled'. (Luke 12:49.) In his mortal life Jesus, the surrendered man, was there only to receive God's love and knew the crushing sorrow of being unable to receive it fully; knew too the sorrow of seeing this same Love, offered to men through him, rejected by them. The humility and poverty which opened them to Love's onrush costs too much. Jesus was ground to death between two millstones: too great Love which humanly he could not receive fully, and too small a love in men which would not receive. In his present and eternal power and glory he remains the same surrendered one but now able to receive fully the weight of Love. What ground him down, broke him open in his earthly condition, now beatifies him. Yet still he suffers anguish, we are told – the Lamb stands slain, the risen Lord bears the marks of his wounding still, scripture bears witness to the fact that something is yet wanting, that there is grief in the Mystery of Love. 'He lives to make intercession for us,' suffering the anguish of his overwhelming love for us, his desire to save us, to give God to us, and the human rejection.

To become Jesus in the mystical marriage is to be taken most deeply into this mystery of passionate Love, to be oneself a vehicle for this Love. Jesus, come to us in the Spirit, living Fire which would burn us up in love, is present in the world only insofar as men and women yield themselves up to him, are transformed in him, become Fire in him. The mystical marriage is not a state of psychic bliss, not a comprehensible fulfilment. It is utterly remote from such paltryness; it has nothing to do with self-states. It is to be with Jesus a total 'for-Godness' which must mean being totally for others; it is an ecstasy of devotedness with no concern for self; it is to be Fire on earth,

117

purifying, enkindling others at a depth far below what we can discern. We have insisted throughout that the direct action of God in the human being is wholly secret. It can be known only by its effects and even these are not easily assessed by 'flesh and blood'. Life hidden with Christ in God' is nourished only by 'life hidden with Christ in God'. It is those who are totally hidden and lost in God, living only with the life of Christ who are Fire on earth.

Banish romantic notions, any high-flown 'spirituality', is Teresa's last word to her reader. Get down to work, eyes fixed on the Crucified, totally devoted to others, regardless of self.

> We should desire and engage in prayer, not for our own enjoyment but for acquiring the strength which fits us for service. Let us not try to walk along an untrodden path, or at the best we shall waste our time.

Thus she leaves us.

> I will end by saying that we must not build towers without foundations, and that the Lord does not look so much at the magnitude of anything we do as to the love with which we do it. If we accomplish what we can, His Majesty will see to it that we become able to do more each day. We must not begin by growing weary; but during the whole of this short life, which for anyone of you may be shorter than you think, we must offer the Lord whatever interior and exterior sacrifice we are able to give Him, and His Majesty will unite it with that which He offered to His Father for us upon the Cross, so that it may have the value won for it by our will, even though our actions in themselves may be trivial.

Diagram showing relation of 'Experiences' or 'Favours' to different stages of prayer in normal (light off) and rare (light on) states

LIGHT OFF
a) *In non-mystical prayer*
i.e. Mansions 1–3

Sensitives

Likely to have them; they are natural in origin, but as they occur in the context of prayer they can be misinterpreted as indicating advanced state. Expectancy of their occurance as also credulity, will heighten likelihood.

Non-sensitives

Unlikely to have them, especially if non-expectant and sceptical by nature.

b) *In mystical prayer*
(Mansion IV (beginners) V & VI

'Experiences' likely, because of natural constitution and other factors of expectancy and credulity. In themselves they are of no significance. But they may have been stimulated by mystical prayer. However, there is no certainty of this, for there is no essential distinction, in regard to 'experiences', between what happens here and what happens in non-mystical prayer.

Unlikely

Mystical prayer, in itself non-experiential (at level of consciousness?), has *always* the effect of imparting *wisdom*, that it, a living knowledge of God which is transforming.

'Experiences' and 'favours' in themselves are *vacuous* in the context of true spiritual wisdom and transformation; whereas mystical prayer is always beneficial, these others may be destructive spiritually and psychologically: they can lead to pride, disorientation and disintegration.

'Light on' does not operate except in mystical prayer for its function is to reveal God in union with the soul. It is a 'seeing' of the actual mystical happening, which as said, is not perceptible to normal range of faculties. It is, it seems, a supernatural endowment which yet (possibly) calls for a natural foundation in which it can operate. This natural foundation could perhaps be classed with 'sensitives' but nevertheless a distinction in the secondary, unimportant effect of 'favours' is observable and thus:

Sensitives
Expectant, credulous:
Experiences and favours abound, especially when they are understood to be what *should* result from God's union with the soul e.g. St Teresa.

The inner 'sight' in itself non-conceptual and therefore incapable of expression, even to the self, is unconsciously given expression to the self, and this expression can be communicated.

As these people are 'sensitives' anyway, and liable to all sorts of psychic experiences, it is likely that this sensitivity will be heightened by the 'sight' they enjoy. Probably they are unable to discern the actual kernel of the grace they are receiving from the

Non-sensitives – or perhaps better to say 'one who is aware of the self's propensity to give form to its inner experience, and therefore avoids doing so: hence absence of phenomena.

There will, however, be absorbtion, ecstasy.

outward shell which is that of their own (unconscious) making: e.g. The visions of St Margaret Mary – she clothed her profound vision with images from her own psyche.

Genuine 'light on' will *always* result in living *wisdom*. The recipients become teachers simply because they actually see what is happening and can tell us about it, thus lighting up what would otherwise lie almost obscured – though not wholly so, for 'light off' too, in the mystical state, really does 'know' what has happened.

There is nothing vacuous about this experience: Note St Teresa's ability to analyse mystical experience; the confidence with which she writes and with which she acts.

It is essentially *transforming*.